GLOUCESTER
A History and Guide

CAROLYN
HEIGHWAY

ALAN SUTTON
1985

Alan Sutton Publishing Limited
Brunswick Road · Gloucester

First published 1985

British Library Cataloguing in Publication Data

Heighway, Carolyn M.
Gloucester : a history and guide.
1. Gloucester (Gloucestershire)—History
I. Title
942.4′14 DA690.G5

ISBN 0-86299-256-7

Cover illustration: I. Harris, Westgate Bridge and the West Gate from the West; *watercolour, 1806. Gloucester City Museum.*

Typesetting and origination by
Alan Sutton Publishing Limited
Printed in Great Britain

Contents

To Richard

Preface and Acknowledgements

A history of Gloucester can be written in many different ways. This is a summary of the main events of Gloucester's past, together with an account of the physical survival of that past in objects and buildings, and some mention of interesting characters. An extensive and detailed history of Gloucester will shortly be available as volume 4 in the *Victoria County History* series.

The section headed 'What to see' is meant to be an indication of the main items; it can be supplemented by the various leaflets available at the Tourist Information Centre. Guided tours are arranged in the summer months by the Civic Trust. Details of historic buildings in Gloucester will be found in D. Verey, *The Buildings of England: Gloucestershire: The Vale and the Forest of Dean* (1970).

I am most grateful to all who have read and commented on drafts of the text or parts of it: Richard Bryant, Arthur Dodd, Brian Frith, Michael Hare, Henry Hurst, Bryan Jerrard, Philip Moss, David Welander, and Malcolm Watkins. I would like to thank Nicholas Herbert, Editor of the Victoria County History for Gloucestershire, who allowed me to read the medieval sections of the forthcoming Gloucester volume. I wish to thank the staff of Gloucester City Museum and Gloucester Folk Museum for their help in finding and loaning illustrations. I am grateful to David Welander for loaning photographs of Gloucester Cathedral. For the late eighteenth and nineteenth centuries the most valuable sources were the Citizen Historical Supplements, published in 1983: the supplements are listed under 'sources', below. I owe a special debt to the staff of the Gloucestershire County Library, Gloucestershire Collection, especially to Jill Voyce, Local History Librarian, for much help and advice on illustrations. Gloucestershire Collection illustrations are annotated *Glos. Coll.*

Note on Measurements and Money

1 mile = 1·6 km

1 foot = about 30 cms

3 feet = 1 yard

1 mark = 6s 8d

1 shilling (s) = 12d (5 new pence)

Roman Gloucester

The Severn Valley in the pre-Roman Iron Age was fertile arable land occupied by many hundreds of farms and settlements. Part of the local tribe, the Dobunni, came to terms with the Roman army soon after the invasion began, so the military occupation of the Gloucester region was a peaceful one. The farmers remained undisturbed, and the soldiers marched down the hill from the east and set up a camp. This camp was not at the site of Gloucester, which remained farmland, but a few kilometres to the north, in what is now a Gloucester suburb called Kingsholm. This is why the Roman road from Cirencester, 'Ermin Street' does not lead straight to the modern town, but has to turn south just outside Gloucester.

This first fort was built in the late 40s or 50s AD. It may have been at a river crossing – until recently Gloucester was the lowest point at which it was possible to bridge or ford the Severn. Certainly the Kingsholm fort was a centre for the further advance of Roman military power into Wales. The Kingsholm fort would have been a rectangular banked enclosure with a grid of streets, timber barracks, and timber gates and towers. It may have been occupied by the Twentieth Legion, although there is no certainty about this, for Legions were often subdivided and posted to more than one station.

Nothing can be seen of this first Roman fort; its remains lie buried under houses and gardens, with its centre under a small green space off Sandhurst Road. Many fittings from the soldiers' armour have been found in this area and can be seen in Gloucester City Museum.

Some years later, in the later 60s AD, the Kingsholm fort was dismantled. A new fortress was placed on a low hill overlooking the river-crossing at Gloucester. It is interesting that the new military unit commissioned its supplies completely independently; its kitchenware pottery was quite different from that of the Kingsholm unit. At the new fortress site, a great clay rampart

The tombstone of Rufus Sita, a cavalryman in the Roman army who died in Gloucester, aged 40, in about 60AD. He was born in Thrace (modern Bulgaria) and joined up at age 18. *Gloucester City Museum.*

Cheekpiece from cavalry helmet, found during archaeological excavations on the site of the first Roman fort at Kingsholm, ½ mile (1 km) north of Gloucester. The decoration depicts Jupiter seated on a throne. *Gloucester City Museum.*

The Roman fortress at Gloucester was founded in the 70s AD on the site of the present town centre. This reconstruction by Richard Bryant shows the east gate of the fortress.

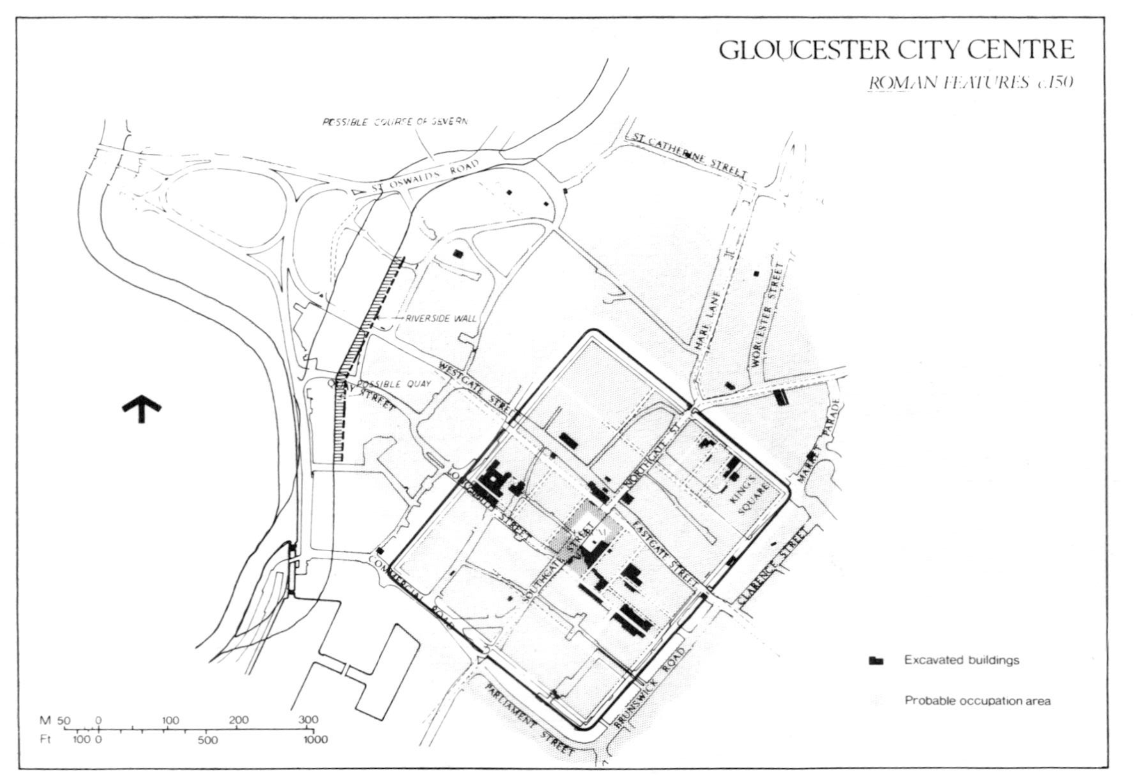

Map of Roman Gloucester in the second century, drawn by Richard Bryant. The town was converted out of the fortress, whose rectangular shape can still be seen. Notice how close the Roman quay was to the town.

Part of a sculpture by David Gillespie Associates showing Roman soldiers in action. The sculpture is on the side of Boots Store, Eastgate Street. *Bill Meadows.*

was built, fronted by blocks of turf, and enclosing a rectangular area of 43 acres (17 hectares). The rampart had wooden gates set in each of the four sides, a wooden walk on top, and watch-towers at intervals. One of the great foot-square timbers which supported towers and gates can be seen in the East Gate display area under Boots Chemists, Eastgate Street, and another can be seen in the City Museum. The timbers were of oak, and many hundreds of trees must have been felled and brought in, probably from the Forest of Dean. To get an idea of the size of the Roman fortress, walk from its East Gate (outside Boots) to the West Gate (close to the 'Roma' cafe in Westgate Street). This fort has left its mark on Gloucester's streets to this day; Parliament Street still joins Brunswick Road in a gentle curve which reflects the 'playing card' shape of the fortress corner, and some main streets, Northgate, Southgate and Eastgate Street, still follow approximately the line laid down by the legionary soldiers almost two thousand years ago.

One arm (now silted up) of the river Severn then flowed close to the town, and, a little downhill from where St. Nicholas church now stands, there was in Roman times a timber quay. Outside the fort there were suburbs of shops and houses for the camp-followers of the soldiers, and also industrial areas, including a tilery north-west of the town. Well beyond the fortress limits were the cemeteries, where soldiers and people were buried, their bodies being cremated and the ashes buried in jars or stone boxes.

After a time, as the Roman conquest of Wales advanced, the legion stationed at Gloucester was moved further west to a new fortress at Caerleon. But the Gloucester fortress was not dismantled, as the Kingsholm one had been; instead it had a surprising future.

The Roman Empire regarded towns as the only true centres of civilization. It was therefore part of Imperial policy to create, in newly conquered areas, towns which would be an example of civilized life, and help to spread Roman ideals. The first such 'colony' in Britain was Colchester, founded in AD 49 (and sacked by Boudicca in 61), the second Lincoln, founded in the late 1st century, and the third Gloucester. At Gloucester the colony was provided with buildings simply by converting the old barrack blocks of the fortress into houses and shops. The new colonists were retired veterans of the Roman army, providing a core of Roman citizens for the new town. The colonists were allocated a plot of land in the countryside as well as a property in the town; they governed the town by electing a council of 100 'decurions' who in turn elected four magistrates; these had responsibility for a wide range of local services.

In Gloucester the initials of several magistrates are stamped on tiles from the municipal factory; the tiles are also stamped RPG for 'Res Publica Glevum' – the equivalent of 'Gloucester City Council'. It would be the magistrates who organised and financed by taxes the rebuilding of the new city; by the second century it had baths, a forum (civic centre), and basilica (town hall). In time the citizens were building fine houses for themselves, with courtyards, piped water, wall paintings, and mosaic floors. One such house was found underneath the site of the Telephone Exchange in Berkeley Street. In the area near the river were several large houses with decorated pavements and wall paintings, like the one buried under the medieval church of St. Mary de Lode. Also in this area was a public building with a

Stamped tile from municipal tilery at St Oswald's Priory. The RPG stands for 'Res Publica Glevum' or 'Gloucester Council'. The other letters are the names of the two magistrates: Julius Florius and Cornelius Similus.

great hall or portico: this is only known to us because it survived to be used as a quarry for the stone to build St. Oswald's Minster, 700 years later. In the Westgate Street area stood the baths, with their great exercise hall supported by columns over 30 feet high. A fragment of one of these can still be seen in the foyer of the City Museum.

In the early second century the town was surrounded by a stone wall to reface the clay rampart which had defended the fortress; the timber gates were also rebuilt in stone. So massive were the gates that they were in use for the next nine hundred years; part of the Roman East Gate can still be seen today. The last remnants of the Roman North Gate were demolished in 1974, and some of the stones from the gate are in the foyer of the National and Provincial Building Society. The Roman riverside suburb was also defended by a stone wall which was still in existence a thousand years later.

The new townspeople were not 'Romans' in the sense that they came from Rome or even Italy; they were Romans by virtue of

Mosaic found on the site of Debenham's store, Northgate Street, in 1955. Many Roman mosaics have been found in Gloucester. They are often very damaged, where later generations have dug their wells and rubbish pits through the underlying Roman floors. *Gloucester City Museum.*

Roman citizenship, and the men had been recruited from all parts of the Empire. They spoke and wrote Latin, but many must have campaigned in Britain and had British families. Most would have picked up some British speech. The name of the new colony, 'Glevum', may be derived from a British word meaning 'bright'.

The Roman town in the second century was densely built up, and included extensive suburbs. The second century town had cemeteries placed, like those of the fortress, about 1 km (half a mile) to the north of the town; cemeteries were, by Roman law, always placed outside town limits, so it is clear that the City Council saw their authority as extending well beyond the walls of the original fortress area. Burial fashions were changing from cremation to inhumation, and many Roman skeletons have been found in the Kingsholm area.

The Roman East Gate was rebuilt in stone in the 2nd century. This reconstruction by Richard Bryant gives an idea of the scale of the gate, which survived until the Norman Conquest. Part of it can still be seen.

The Roman East Gate, excavated in 1974, looking east. *Gloucester City Museum Excavation Unit.*

This Roman column was found during the building of the Midland Bank, 4 Westgate Street, in 1971 and was transferred by crane to the Museum: it now stands in the foyer. The base on which the column rested is in the bank window. A number of similar columns have been found on the north side of Westgate Street and the street (which is not Roman) may have been created because the columns marked a way through the ruined Roman town. *By courtesy of 'The Citizen', Gloucester.*

Archaeological excavations at 11–17 Berkeley Street, on the corner of Longsmith Street, in 1971, during the building of the Telephone Exchange. Just in front of the digging machine is a Roman building. It was one of the bonuses of redevelopment that archaeologists gained an opportunity to record the past of Gloucester before it was built over: much of the information on the maps in this book derives from excavations such as this one. *Gloucester City Museum Excavation Unit.*

The new town stimulated trade and industry; the rebuilding itself created jobs; the increased population provided a market for local goods; the demand for Roman fashions in kitchenware promoted the establishment of pottery industries. Pottery was also imported on a large scale from Dorset. For every day table-ware the citizens used the glossy red pottery imported from France and known today as 'samian'; the rich, for special dinner parties, would have tables laden with pewter or silver.

The recurrent political crises of the Roman Empire impinged on the towns from time to time, and it may have been the civil war between Albinus and Severus which prompted many towns to build earthwork defences, in the late second century. At Gloucester a great bank of soil was piled behind the stone walls, and a series of stone watch-towers added.

Gloucester by the fourth century was a very different place to the new colony of the second. The vast increase in the cost of imperial administration tended to deflect attention from the towns; the financial burden for town magistrates was now considerable, and people avoided the office if they could. In Gloucester, expenditure on public buildings went down. Parts of the great baths complex were divided up and sub-let as small industrial units. There is little evidence of great new buildings on the scale of two hundred years before. The town limit, beyond which the cemeteries appeared, moved inwards, suggesting that the town boundaries had been redrawn to a smaller compass. The town could still muster expenditure on a grand scale, for in the early fourth century the defences were refurbished, the gates altered, a length of wall rebuilt on either side of the gates, a new wide ditch dug, and a series of round or polygonal wall-towers added to the outside of the wall. The purpose of the towers was to mount stone ballistas or catapults. Since the ballistas required special military skills, it may also suggest that there was a military unit billeted in the town. The defensive measures show that the town was capable of concerted effort, and that it was thought worth defending.

This was the last major Roman work on the defences. In what remained of the century the beginnings of economic change occurred which resulted in the end of Roman towns. First there was disruption of the trading network. As the century wore on the pottery industries of Dorset and elsewhere went into decline. In Gloucester ordinary pottery began to come from the east midlands area and not from Dorset. The better tableware was

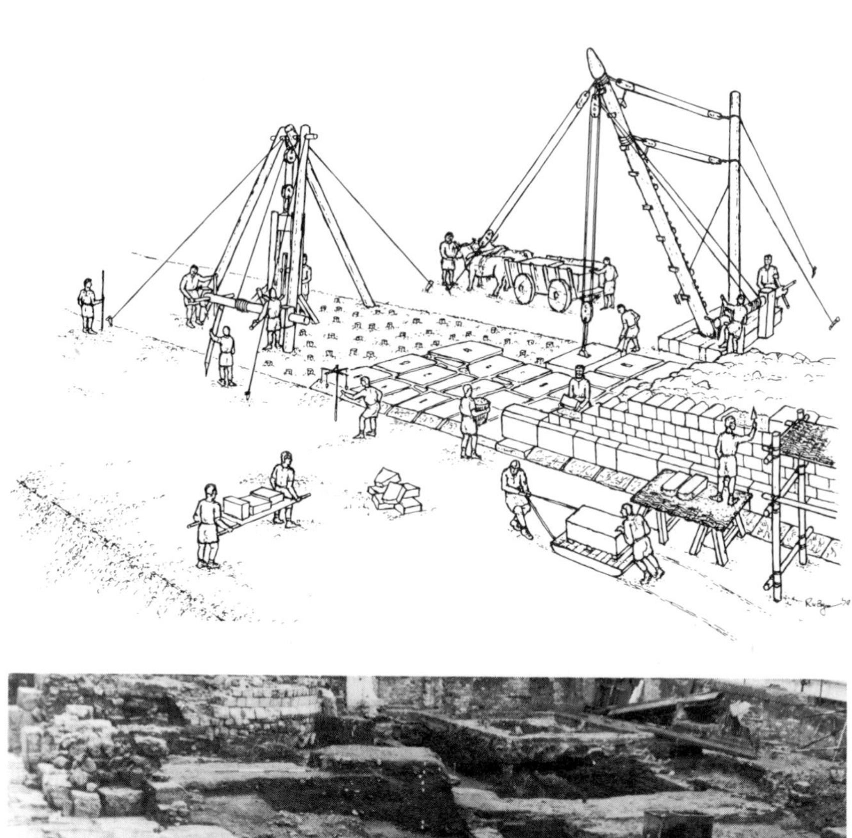

The 4th-century Roman city wall near the East Gate: a drawing by Richard Bryant showing the wall being built. Below is a photograph showing the foundations of the wall, uncovered in 1974. The wall was destroyed during the 18th and 19th centuries. *Gloucester City Museum Excavation Unit.*

now obtained from new centres in Oxfordshire. Continental imports, from Gaul and elsewhere, had long since dwindled to nothing. These changes in markets need not have affected local conditions. There remained rich men in Gloucester; a new tesselated floor in one house was laid at the very end of the century. But new works on great town houses were rare in this century – a contrast to the countryside, where the villas with their mosaic floors and painted walls were enjoying a period of unprecedented prosperity.

At the end of the fourth century, civil wars in the Roman Empire were almost constant, and their effects were worsened by barbarian raids from outside the Empire. The British garrisons had been many times depleted to take part in the Emperors' dynastic struggles, and there were no troops to spare when Saxons attacked Britain in 409. At this point the British organised their own defence. There was probably every expectation that the Roman administrators and military would one day return; but this did not happen. This was the end of Roman Britain.

A real blow to Gloucester's prosperity was the end of the money economy. Coin had always circulated because it was used to pay the army; when the final army unit was withdrawn, the money supply ceased. For a few decades coin continued to be used, but it seems to have stopped circulating by about 450. Lack of coinage was not the only destructive factor. Worsening climate, resulting in poorer harvests, coupled with the lack of the military market, also had an effect. In the early fifth century life in at least one Gloucester house (under the present Eastgate

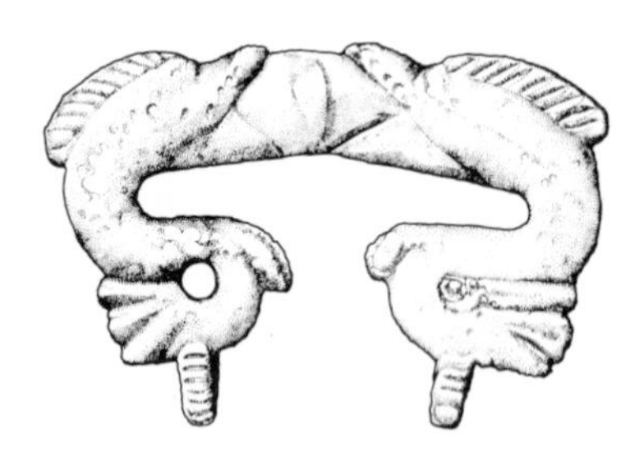

A late-Roman 'dolphin' belt-buckle, found at a Roman farm at Saintbridge near Gloucester. These buckles have been found in the town too: they are supposed to have belonged to British soldiers – a sort of Home Guard. The cities of Britain were defending themselves. *Drawing: D. Owen.*

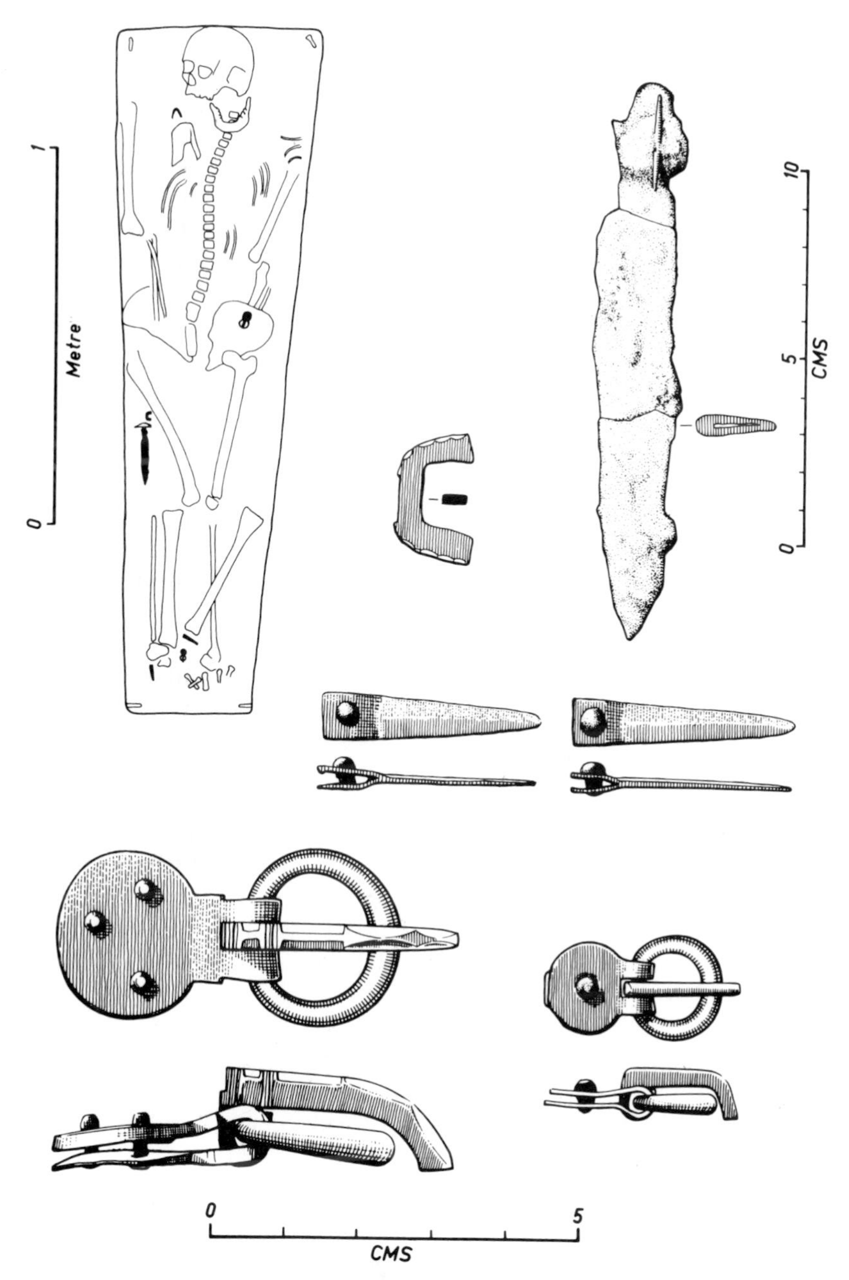

The burial of a warrior at Kingsholm in the early 5th century. The objects imply that the man was British, and since he was buried in a special building, he must have been a man of rank. *Drawing: Phil Moss.*

market) still continued, but in time the occupants left. The house decayed and the roof fell in, collapsing onto the floor and bringing with it a coin hoard which had been hidden in the roof in the early 400s.

However, some town organisation continued. There was a major replanning of the centre of Gloucester in about 410; the great forum courtyard at the town centre was extended to the north. The baths were demolished and levelled over and timber buildings put up on the platforms created by the debris. These buildings could have had quite grand classical facades, of the type now known to have existed at Wroxeter at the same date. Some sort of local military unit was probably in existence: late-Roman 'dolphin' belt buckles found in Gloucester and on sites close to the town indicate British levies – a sort of Home Guard. There were warrier leaders as well. In the early 400s, a British warrior of high rank was buried at Kingsholm cemetery with his weapons. His body was placed in a special stone chamber or mausoleum. This cemetery may have stayed in use in the centuries to come, and may have been remembered when the Saxon palace was constructed on its site in the tenth century.

Urban life thus continued for some decades after the 'end of Roman Britain', but in the end economic disruption was too great, and the town became ruinous. Much of the urban area became arable land; in some areas manure and soil was brought in to make it more fertile. Two hundred years after the end of Roman rule, the city was still seen as a centre of its region, so it is likely that somewhere in the town there remained regional administrators. Pottery of the fifth or sixth century, and a collection of smith's tools of the same date, have been found. There were obviously people in the town, but Roman Gloucester was at an end.

ROMAN GLOUCESTER: WHAT TO SEE

- The Roman East Gate and Roman city wall: can be viewed in the gallery under Boots Chemists, Eastgate Street. Access at the side of the store. For opening times inquire at City Museum.

- City Museum, Brunswick Road: Roman objects, mosaics, and 4th-century wall.

- Gloucester Furniture Exhibition Centre, on the corner of Parliament Street and Southgate Street: city wall; access by appointment only.

- Westgate Street: Roman finds on display in Williams and Glyn's Bank (No. 1), Midland Bank (No. 4), Alliance Building Society (No. 30).

- St. Mary de Lode Church: Roman mosaic can be viewed under trap-door in nave floor.

- Roman North Gate: stones from this in the foyer of the National and Provincial Building Society, 45–9 Northgate Street.

British Kingdom to Saxon Town: 450–800

It used to be thought that the Anglo-Saxon invasions destroyed Romano-British towns; the case of Gloucester (amongst others) shows that this was not so. The Anglo-Saxon invasions of England began about 400 in the south-east of the country and continued for 200 years; Gloucester was not conquered until 577. Yet by then it was a town no longer.

The Severn Valley was probably reasonably prosperous, and would have been governed and defended by a military elite, led by warrior chieftians. In the early 500s, the chieftain of the Gloucester area may have been called Conan; by 577 there was a successor, Conmail. The province was no doubt Christian; having close contacts with the Christian Kingdoms of south Wales where saints such as David and Samson flourished. Christianity had been the official religion in the fourth-century Empire and the Vale of Gloucester had suffered no disturbance which need have eradicated it.

A survival of Christianity makes it likely that the church of St. Mary de Lode in Gloucester has its origins as a small Christian burial oratory, in turn related to part of a wealthy Roman house. At St. Mary de Lode, excavations showed that after the Roman house (a grand one, with mosaics and wall-paintings) was demolished, a timber building on the same alignment was built on the ruins. Inside this building were several burials, facing east in the Christian manner. They cannot be dated closely, but a post-Roman date is certain (no Roman town would bury its dead inside the walls). Much later, St. Mary's became a parish church, and was appropriated to the Abbey of St. Peter, but it can be claimed that the eighteenth-century antiquaries were right, and that St. Mary de Lode is on the site of an early British church.

In 577 Gloucester was occupied by an Anglo-Saxon army; in the words of the Anglo-Saxon Chronicle: 'In this year Cuthwine and Ceawlin fought against the Britons and killed three kings, Conmail, Condidan, and Farinmail, at the place which is called

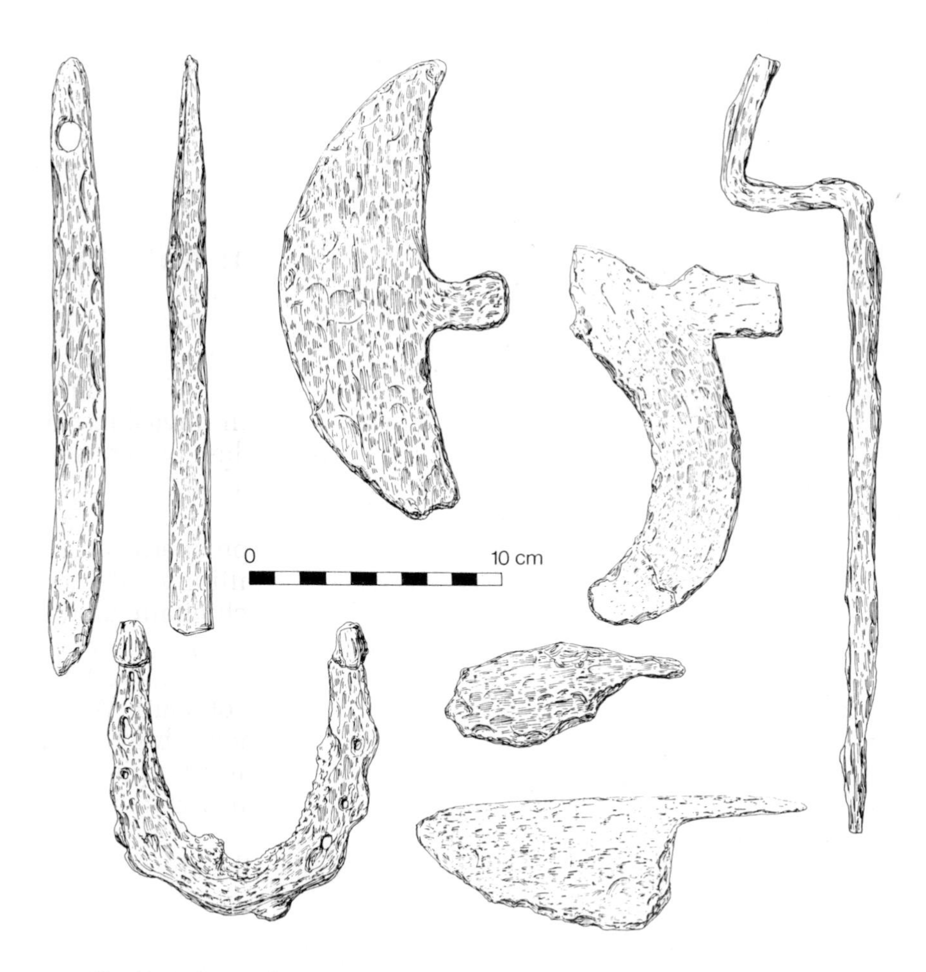

A collection of iron objects, mostly smiths' tools, found during excavations in Commercial Road in 1983. These tools date to the 6th century and show that Gloucester was still occupied after Roman rule ceased. *Drawing: Damyon Rey.*

Dyrham; and they captured three of their cities, Gloucester, Cirencester, and Bath.' This conquest probably records at random one of a number of complicated political squabbles (it is notable that the leaders of the 'Saxon' army have Celtic names). Archaeological evidence shows that the few Saxons who had entered the Gloucestershire area by 577 had come from the Thames Valley direction, whereas the annal suggests conquest from Wessex and the south. After 577 a kingdom, subordinate to

Gloucester in 681; a painting by Richard Bryant. The Roman North Gate (top of picture) and Roman walls still stand. Ruined Roman buildings can be seen including (bottom right) the basilica (town hall). A few wealthy citizens have salvaged enough Roman tiles to re-roof surviving Roman houses, while most of the inhabitants have built thatched, half-timbered halls and cottages among the ruins. Outside the walls more fields extend over what were once the Roman suburbs. Westgate Street

(bottom centre) has been formed and passes between the columns of a Roman public building. The Roman forum has become a cattle market. Much of the town is under cultivation. The newly-founded Abbey is on the left: there is a small stone church and two enclosures with halls: one each for monks and nuns. There is a preaching-cross in the churchyard.

the kingdom of Wessex, was established in the lower Severn Valley. In 628 the Mercians defeated the West Saxons at the battle of Cirencester, and it was probably at this time that the kingdom of the Hwicce came into existence, a kingdom corresponding broadly to the counties of Gloucestershire and Worcestershire. The Hwicce were from their origins subordinate to the great kingdom of Mercia. Until the sixteenth century, the boundaries of this kingdom survived as the limits of the diocese of

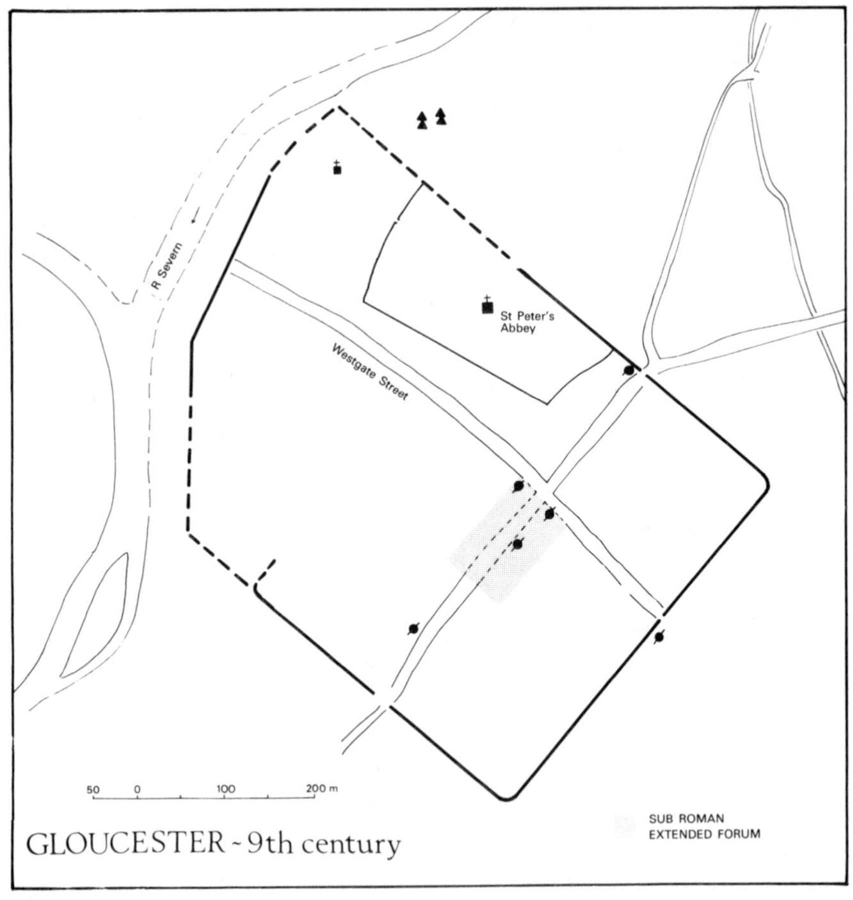

Map suggesting the layout of Gloucester in the 9th century. Almost no Roman streets have survived, except where they passed out through the north and east gates. Westgate Street has moved north from its Roman line, and the Roman forum extended north also. The round symbols show where 9th-century pits have been found. The double triangles represent 9th-century sculpture.

A key from Gloucester, decorated with animal heads, possibly 9th century. *Gloucester City Museum.*

Worcester. Political power was essential to the spread of the Anglo-Saxon church, and when the diocese of Worcester was created in 679 it was natural that the boundary should be the same as that of the kingdom of the Hwicce.

If, at the arrival of the Anglo-Saxon power, Gloucester was already Christian, it was a different brand of Christianity, and the ruling nobility saw it as their duty to reorganise the Christianity of their new territory. To do this, they founded new churches, 'minsters', in many major centres. At Gloucester, *c.* 679, Osric, King of the Hwicce, founded a monastery church dedicated to St. Peter. He had also founded a minster at Bath, a few years earlier, also dedicated to St. Peter. It is interesting that the key towns of 577 seems to have been the centres where it was thought right to put the new churches; however deserted these places were, they retained some regional significance.

Gloucester, like Bath, was one of a number of 'double monasteries', houses for women, but with provision for men who were needed to carry out the pastoral work. One important aspect of these monasteries was that the leaders and some inmates were aristocrats; thus the monastery was not only a centre of piety and learning but also had political influence. Judging by complaints made in the next century, many monks and nuns were given to wearing fine silks and furs, employing musicians and harpists, and drinking alchohol, sometimes in unseemly quantities. This was only to be expected; rank was the most important aspect of Anglo-Saxon society. Those who took up the religious life did not necessarily expect to dispense with the luxuries which they thought of as theirs by right of birth. At Gloucester the monastery was run by Osric's sister Kyneburgh; no doubt she looked after her brother's political interests in the region, as well as attending to the service of God.

It is not known what this early monastery at Gloucester looked like, but it probably had a stone church, and two enclosed areas of buildings, one each for men and women. The great cathedral of today sprawls across the Roman fortress wall, but the church of 679 was probably tucked into the corner of the Roman fortress area.

When Osric founded the new monastery, he was given 'the land of three hundred tributaries' to provide the new foundation with income. The 'tributarius' was a Roman land tax, and the use of the word in 679 may indicate that a Roman system of administration continued in Gloucester beyond the Saxon conquest.

The new monastery helped attract settlers and craftsmen to the town. The monastery church would have been decorated with painted stone sculpture, embroidered hangings, and precious objects; all this must be imagined, as none of it has survived. The town was still a very small settlement, dominated by the larger of the Roman ruins. A new street (today called Westgate Street) had by now been created through the central colonnade of a Roman public building. The column in the foyer of the City Museum is part of this colonnade.

The loss of the Roman street grid shows how much the Roman town had decayed. Only three main routes occupy Roman streets and this is an accident; all routes through the town had to pass through the gates, and so some of the main streets were kept in being. The eastern boundary of the Abbey in 679 was laid out on a Roman street, and so has roughly preserved the Roman line in St. John's Lane. Otherwise the Roman street grid has dis-

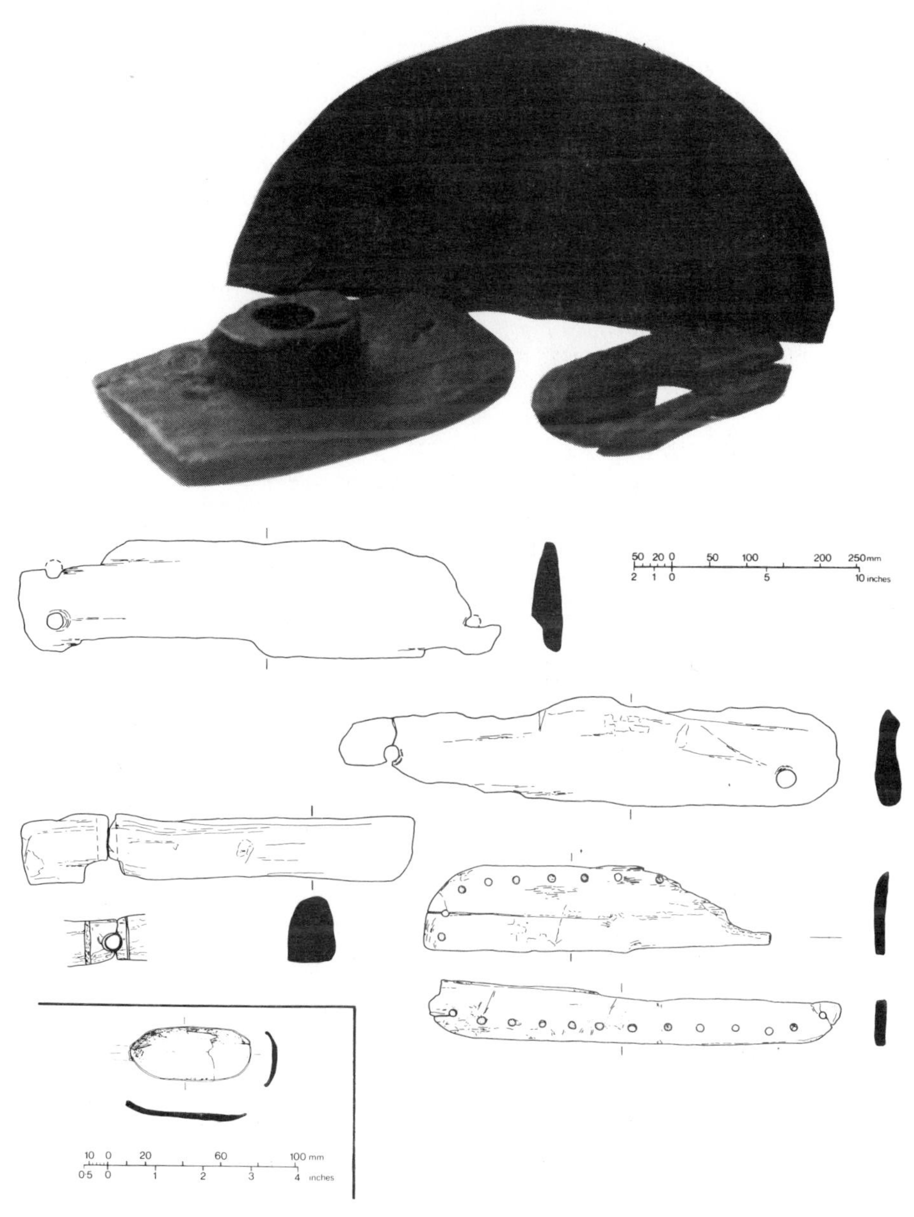

9th-century wooden objects from excavations at 1, Westgate Street. Nearly everything in the 800s was made of wood: cups, bowls, spoons, furniture, and tools. Seen here are the lid from a barrel, a churn paddle, and a rope-wood (part of the tackle of a ship). The barrel-cover measures 1 ft. 1 in. (330mm) in diameter. Below are drawings of pieces of furniture, a spoon, and a basket-base.

Part of the shaft of a standing cross found at St Oswald's Priory. Two more cross-shafts have been found built into the ruin of c.900, and all the shafts must date to the 9th century. *Drawing: Richard Bryant.*

appeared, and the present regular pattern is a product of a later age – that of Alfred the Great.

All this time Gloucester was still populated, although it can hardly be called a town. Some excavations at Westgate Street, underneath William and Glyn's bank, gave a glimpse of everyday life in the town in the 800s. By chance, a pile of rubbish and animal dung, quickly buried, had preserved many things which usually decay rapidly. A large piece of cloth from a woman's dress had been woven on an upright loom. One of these looms would have stood in every Saxon household. With the cloth were broken fragments of the ring-shaped clay weights which held down the warps. Also in the dung-heap were fragments of wooden objects; barrel staves, spoons, bowls and cups, pieces of furniture, buckets, and a churn-paddle. Pieces of leather off-cuts from shoes showed that a cobbler was working close to the site; he had acquired a nobleman's sword-scabbard to cut up and re-use.

This glimpse of Anglo-Saxon life is a reminder of what is missing, for nearly everything used by these people was made of wood. Cooking was done in iron cauldrons or very occasionally, in pots brought from another county. Houses too were wooden, though they could be substantial. By contrast, magnificent stone crosses were put up in the 800s on the site later occupied by St. Oswald's Priory: this shows that somewhere in the town, there were aristocrats with money to spend on monuments of the highest quality.

There is nothing about any of the objects mentioned above to show that the activity concerned is not in the depths of the countryside. It is surprising that there was no trace of smithing, iron-working, or even the use of iron nails. Iron working was common in the late Roman town, and in the eleventh century. Whatever else it was, a market or an administrative centre, there is nothing particularly town-like about Gloucester in the 800s.

FIFTH TO NINTH CENTURY: WHAT TO SEE

- Reconstruction painting of 7th-century Gloucester: exhibition in the Gallery of Gloucester Cathedral.

- Pagan Saxon objects: display in Gloucester City Museum, Brunswick Road.

- 9th-century stone cross-shafts from the site of St. Oswald's Priory; stone cross-shaft from Wotton Pitch, just north of Gloucester; in City Museum.

- 9th-century loom weight; leather objects: display in Gloucester City Museum.

A Tenth-century New Town

In this year a great [Danish] naval force came over here . . . from Britanny. And they then went west round the coast so that they arrived at the Severn Estuary and ravaged in Wales. . . . Then . . . the army went inland. . . . Then the men from Hereford and Gloucester and from the nearest boroughs met them and fought against them and put them to flight and killed . . . a great part of the army.

So the Anglo-Saxon Chronicle reports part of a successful defence against one of the great Danish armies. A Danish army had already wintered in Gloucester in 877, but no battle is then recorded (one Chronicler says they 'built booths in the streets'). In 914 the situation was very different; the town of Gloucester, among others, was organised for defence, and organised well.

The refortification of the towns of western Mercia, part of an in-depth defence against the Danes, was organised by Aethelflaed of Mercia, daughter of Alfred the Great. The towns, Gloucester, Hereford, Bridgnorth, Tamworth and many others, were fortified or re-fortified and laid out with a grid of streets. The Saxons called these fortified centres 'burhs'. Often new religious foundations went hand-in-hand with these new towns, whose purpose was twofold, to be military strongholds, and commercial centres. Gloucester still had its Roman walls, including the riverside wall, and some of its Roman gates. These, it is assumed, were repaired where necessary. The streets were relaid within the Roman walls, the aim being both to lay out plots for commercial use, and to provide easy access to the walls in time of danger. There was also a street just inside the walls. This street pattern is similar to that of many of Alfred's towns, particularly Winchester, dated to the late ninth century. In Berkeley Street, a telephone inspection trench cut through a remarkable layer-cake of superimposed streets, dating from the thirteenth century back to the tenth; from under the third street

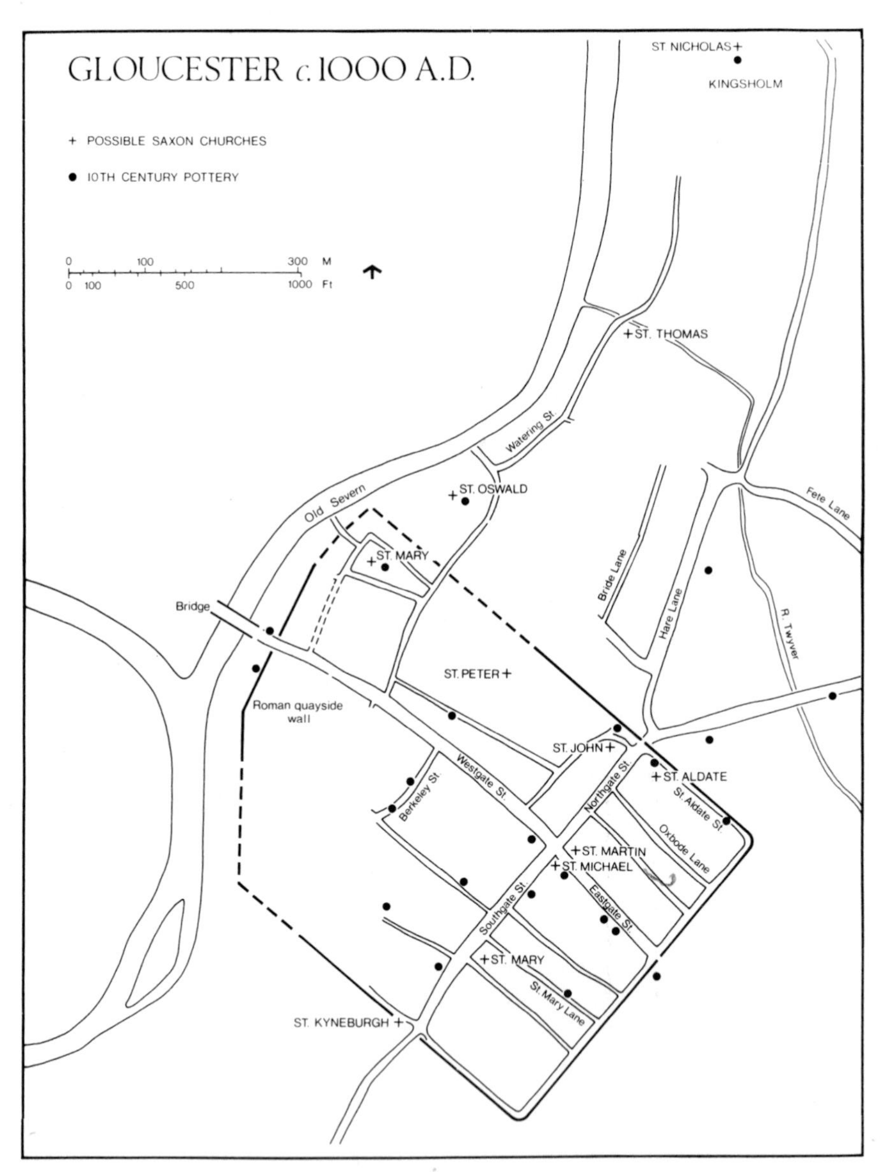

Map of Gloucester in the 10th century. The streets are more or less those of today: they are thought to have been planned by Aethelflaed, daughter of Alfred, as part of a system of refortification during the Danish wars. The circle symbols show where 10th-century pottery has been found and so indicate where people were living. The bridge was near the later Foreign Bridge: the 'Old Severn' branch of the river later silted up and was only a culvert by the post-medieval period. *Drawing: Phil Moss.*

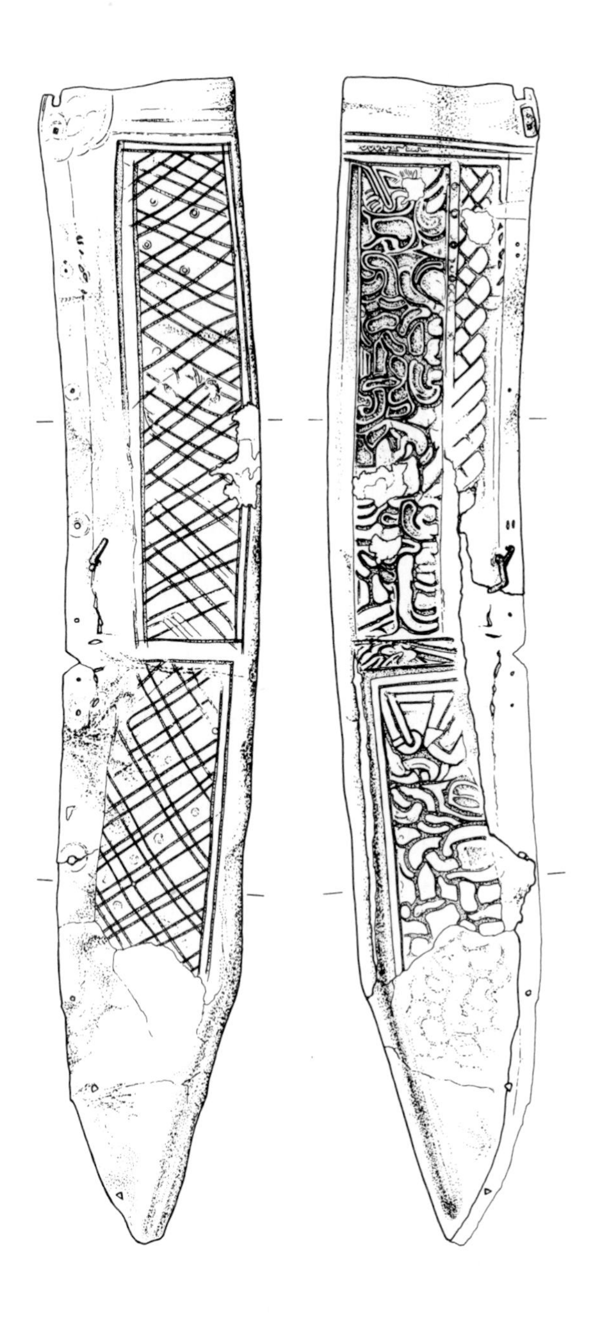

Leather scramasax sheath, 10th or 11th century, found on one of the earliest surfaces of Berkeley Street. The scramasax was a cross between a sword and a knife. *Drawing: Richard Bryant.*

from the bottom came a 'scramasax' sheath which once contained the sword of a Saxon thegn. It appears that by the time Berkeley Street was laid out, the western wall of the Roman fortress, which runs under it, had been at least partly demolished.

The western limit of the Saxon town was the old river course, a few dozen yards west of the Roman quayside. The river may have been bridged or forded. The medieval bridge at this point was called 'Foreign Bridge' (Outer Bridge) which means it once marked the town boundary.

The western part of the town, still protected by the Roman riverside wall, contained some important buildings. Here was to be found the ancient church of St. Mary de Lode, and a little north of that, the minster of St. Oswald. This was a church founded by Aethelflaed of Mercia not long before 900 AD, about the time when the new 'burh' of Gloucester was being created.

The church today consists of a single ruined wall which incorporates many different periods of architecture from the sixteenth century back to the tenth. The large blocks high up in the wall are remnants of the church built by Aethelflaed *c.* 900. This first church was quite small and conservative in plan except for two elements which denote influence from the great Carolingian buildings of the Continent: a western apse, and a separate pillared eastern crypt. The crypt is the type in which a secular ruler might be buried, and it may have been built for Aethelflaed herself: she died in 918. The chronicle, in stating that she was buried in St. Peter's Abbey, may be referring to St. Oswald's, for it is not known to which saint Aethelflaed's church was originally dedicated. The church was already in existence when, in 909, important relics were brought there, snatched out of Danish territory in Bardney, Lincs, during a raid led by Aethelflaed and her brother Edward, King of Wessex. The bones of St. Oswald, seventh-century king and saint, were laid to rest in the New Minster at Gloucester.

The church was built partly using stone re-used from a great Roman public building. The church was richly decorated with stone sculpture, elaborately carved and painted in bright colours; there was a great wall-painting at the crossing arch; there would also have been embroidered hangings, and reliquaries, book-covers, and other furniture such as censers or candlesticks in gold, silver and jewels. Viewed in candlelight in the semi-darkness, for the church had few windows, the church would

St Oswald's minster: a model made by Richard Bryant. The stones drawn on the model show all that remains above ground of the church built by Aethelflaed of Mercia, c.900. The church had a western apse, and a separate eastern crypt with pillars: both inspired by Continental buildings. East is on the left.

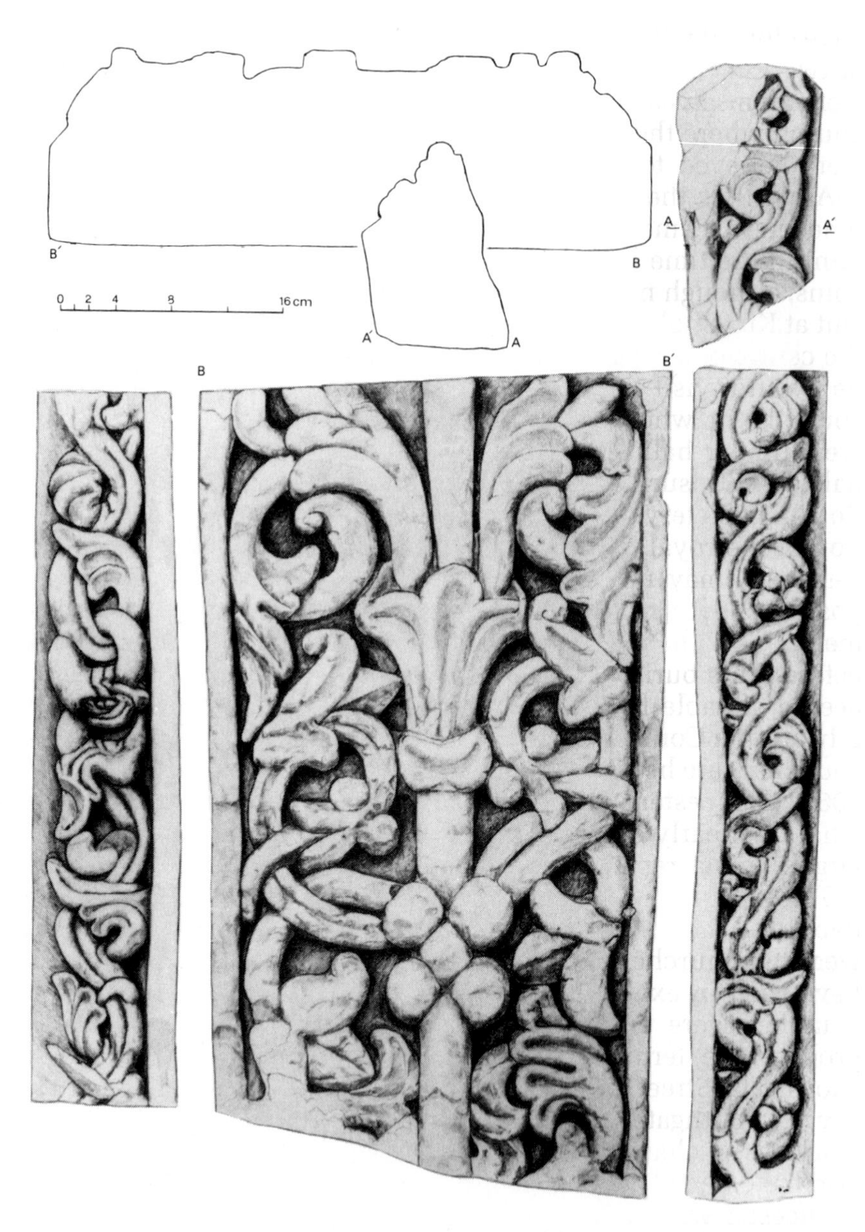

An early 10th-century grave-cover from St Oswald's Priory. Richly decorated, once painted, it belonged to the tomb of a person of rank, possibly Queen Aethelflaed herself. *Drawing: Richard Bryant.*

have glowed with richness. Such treasures are now lost; only one or two fragments hint at their presence. The relics of St. Oswald were themselves a great treasure, and pilgrims flocked to visit the church where the saint was laid, and to seek the cures his relics were believed to bring.

As well as the new minster of St. Oswald, the town acquired other new elements in the tenth century. It had already had a mint in the time of Alfred, and must have continued to produce coins, although none of the early tenth century have been found. Out at Kingsholm, about half-a-mile north of the town, there was the centre of a royal manor, one of the king's own estates which he would visit from time to time, either when convening councils, or when hunting in the Forest of Dean. There was a great timber hall here in the tenth and eleventh centuries. The hall and its surrounding buildings were on the site of a late Roman cemetery, which has already been mentioned. The location of the royal manor and its chapel, in the same spot as this cemetery, may not be accidental; the Roman mausoleum was possibly still standing in the 900s, or there may have been a memory of the ancient burial ground of five hundred years before. This burial ground, for people of high rank, would have been a suitable focus for the royal manor of later centuries. In Edward the Confessor's time, the great hall at Kingsholm, where councils were held, was known as a palace. A Mercian council of 896 at Gloucester may have been held at the Kingsholm hall, and a hoard of early eleventh-century coins from Kingsholm was so large it must represent the taxes of a wide region.

Tenth-century Gloucester had other churches as well as the two great minsters of St. Peter and St. Oswald. By 1100 there were ten churches in the town and at least some of these must have been in existence in the tenth century. These early urban churches were tiny, and had no burial grounds. They should probably be termed chapels rather than churches. St. John's (Northgate Street), St. Michael (at the Cross), and St. Mary de Crypt (Southgate Street) are probably on the site of Saxon churches. A chapel of St. Michael's, dedicated to St. Martin, may also have been Saxon. Many Saxon towns had gate chapels, and Gloucester was no exception; the little chapel of St. Kyneburgh was situated on the site of the Roman South Gate, and may even have been converted out of the Roman gate itself. Nothing remains of St. Kyneburgh's today and its site is buried beneath modern roads.

A stone bear's head, probably Anglo-Saxon, found on the site of All Saints Church, at the Cross. *Gloucester Museum Excavation Unit.*

Another tiny church was All Saints, which stood near the central crossroads of the town. It measured 35 by 18 feet, and occupied just one house plot, with its chancel jutting out into the street. Excavations of the church in 1893 produced a stone bear's head of Anglo-Saxon date, now in the City Museum.

The only real parish church of the town was the old Minster of St. Peter, founded four hundred years before. The old church was the place where nearly everyone in the town, and in the territory round about, was buried. The only other churches which had, by this date, acquired the right of burial (which was a source of income) were St. Oswald and St. Mary de Lode. Too little is known about the history of St. Peter's Abbey. It is probably not true that it had to be refounded in the eighth century; gifts to it were continuous. It can be assumed that like most other Saxon churches, it was full of treasures, and was a small if complex structure. It may have stood in the area south of the present Cathedral. In 1022 St. Peter's was reformed, that is, its priests were pensioned off or told to put away their wives, and a community of monks, living under strict Benedictine rule, was substituted. In 1058 Ældred, Bishop of Worcester and later Archbishop of York, rebuilt the Abbey on a new site, perhaps under the present cathedral. It was this new abbey which, less than three decades later, was burnt down and replaced with the enormous Norman structure which still survives today. It is surprising that there are no fragments of Gloucester's great Saxon Abbey. The crypt of the Cathedral is sometimes held to be late Saxon, but this is doubted by most art historians.

The visiting pilgrims, both to St. Oswald's and to the old minster of St. Peter, the new town organisation, the presence of a royal mint, a royal hall; all these would have helped to create a flourishing town and market. The town was becoming more built-up, with substantial timber-framed buildings, sometimes cellared, on the frontage of the main streets. There were craft workers in the town; not only weavers and cobblers who were to be found everywhere, but also potters, glass-workers, and silversmiths. There would also have been woodturners, coopers and smiths. Gloucester in the tenth century was a busy place, yet it was by no means fully inhabited. Only along the main streets were there houses, stalls and workshops.

Royal visits, with their train of nobles with purchasing power, were a bonus, in spite of the fact that one of the duties of the townsfolk was to provide some of the food and other necessities for the royal visit. The chronicles mention few royal visits to Gloucester in the tenth century; perhaps they were routine, and were noted only when an event of particular note took place, for example the death of King Æthelstan in Gloucester in 939. In the eleventh century there seems to have been great improvement in Gloucester's prosperity, perhaps because of the frequent visits of Edward the Confessor, whose Council was convened at Gloucester nine times between 1043 and 1062. The councils were probably held at the Kingsholm palace.

It was in the eleventh century that the amount and variety of manufactured goods, in particular pottery, increased. By the eleventh century if not before, Gloucester's iron working trade was important again, and Gloucester's render to the crown was in iron nails and bars.

Gloucester still had military and strategic importance. In 1051 Edward the Confessor assembled forces at Gloucester against Godwine's revolt; in 1055 Earl Ælfgar allied with Irish and Welsh forces and sacked and burnt Hereford; to counteract this a national force was assembled by Harold Godwineson (later King Harold) at Gloucester. Peace was in time made with Ælfgar without further fighting. Another expedition against the Welsh, again organised by Harold from Gloucester, took place in 1063.

Gloucester thus still controlled an important route into Wales. It also formed a focal point in the national network of Anglo-Saxon military and civil administration, for it had, by the eleventh century, become a shire town, and this may have been another cause, rather than an effect, of further economic growth. Why Gloucester was chosen, and not Cirencester, or Winchcombe, is not known; there were no doubt political reasons which are now lost. The importance of Gloucester's Roman past may have been a factor. As a shire-town, Gloucester was the administrative centre for the group of hundreds which comprised the shire. Here would have been held the shire court; from here the king's sheriff (shire reeve) would manage local finance and local justice. By 1086, Gloucester was a flourishing small town with mint, market and famous churches, as well as that most important attribute, burgage tenure, the early version of freehold property which made possible a lively property market in the towns and enabled them to move forward on the path to independence.

TENTH TO ELEVENTH CENTURIES: WHAT TO SEE

- St. Oswalds Priory: stones in standing wall and one arch are of Saxon work.

- 10th-century sculpture from St. Oswalds in City Museum, Brunswick Road.

- Street pattern of present day Gloucester is 10th-century.

- Sculpture, roundel of Christ, in Cathedral Gallery Expedition, date 10th-century or Romanesque; its date is disputed.

- 11th-century wooden objects and pottery on display in City Museum, Brunswick Road.

Castle and Abbey: 1066–1200

In 1066, as is well-known, William of Normandy successfully mounted a military campaign to stake his claim to the English throne. Gloucester was not one of the few centres which organised resistance to William. The most significant change was the new ownership of the land. The old Saxon nobility was dispossessed or killed and it was now Norman tenants-in-chief who owned the 'ground rent' of the town properties. The principal overlord was William Fitz-Osbern, Earl of Hereford, who controlled most of the West of England. Early in William's reign, Roger de Pîtres was appointed Sheriff of Gloucestershire and Constable of Gloucester Castle; this Roger was founder of a family which dominated Gloucester history in the next few decades – the 'Gloucester family'.

To ordinary people, the new lords may have made little difference; most noticeable would have been the great new buildings which the Normans imposed on the town. A castle was the first, and the most important; it ensured the control of the town and thus of the surrounding countryside. Gloucester castle was a 'motte-and-bailey', an earthen mound surmounted by a wooden tower, with a defended enclosure (the bailey) beside it. The fact that the castle constable was also Sheriff, or revenue collecter for the town and county, was a good way of controlling revenues by a show of military force.

In a rubbish-pit of the castle was a gaming-board and full set of thirty counters from the game known as 'tables' – an early version of Backgammon. This set was a luxury object which could have belonged to the Constable's household.

The Normans also rebuilt some of the town gates. The Roman East Gate was demolished and rebuilt except for its front wall which was incorporated in the new gate. The North Gate was similarly rebuilt, and perhaps the West and South Gates as well.

The new lords were ecclesiastical as well as secular. The new Abbot of Gloucester Abbey, Serlo, was appointed in 1072; the

The East Gate after its rebuilding by the Normans c. 1080. The Roman gate was mostly demolished, except for one wall, incorporated in the new gate. *Drawing: Richard Bryant.*

numbers in the Abbey were down to two monks and eight novices, and some of the Abbey's possessions had been appropriated by York. Serlo's energy must have been remarkable; by 1100 he had increased his numbers to 100 monks, and he had begun the great new Abbey Church which is now Gloucester Cathedral. The Anglo-Saxon building had been burnt in 1088, but in any case it had probably been a church in the Anglo-Saxon style, and therefore too small for Norman tastes. The foundation stone of a new Abbey was laid in 1089, and the building dedicated in 1100, although at that date only the east end was completed. The west end and the claustral buildings, where the monks lived, took some years more, and in 1110 some more land had to be bought from St. Oswald's Priory to

Part of set of the game of 'Tables' (similar to Backgammon) found in a rubbish pit of the first castle. The set is a luxury item, with all its 30 pieces and board complete. It is hard to see why it should have been thrown away. Did a player lose his temper? *Western Archaeological Trust and Gloucester Museum.*

Gloucester's first castle as it might have appeared c. 1080, viewed from the east. The castle was a symbol of the military power of the Norman conquerors. *Based on a drawing by Damyon Rey.*

accommodate all the new buildings. This Abbey is the most magnificent structure that the Normans have bequeathed to modern Gloucester. A substantial amount of it survives today, though often hidden behind later perpendicular additions. The church has the great columnar nave typical of the West Country school of Norman church building (Tewkesbury is another example); but Gloucester is unique in having three identical storeys: at each level, crypt, ground floor, and triforium, there is an ambulatory with radiating chapels.

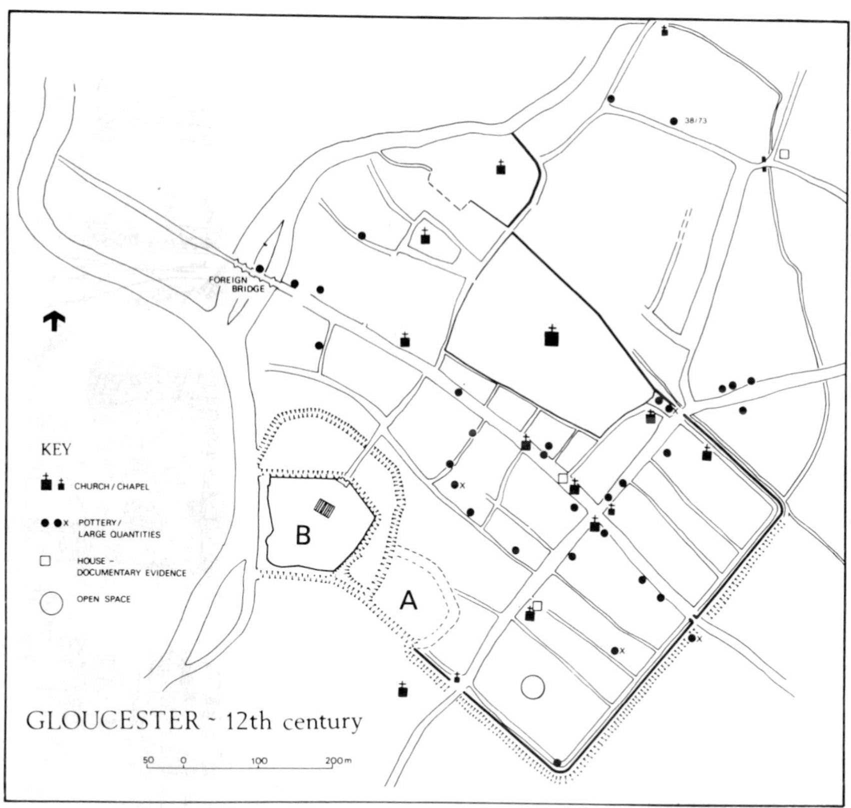

Gloucester in the 12th century. Castle and abbey have made their mark on the town, and finds of pottery (round symbols) show the town is more densely occupied than a century before. A: position of first castle, B: position of later (stone) castle.

The Anglo-Saxon tradition of the royal crown-wearing in the three centres of Winchester, Westminster, and Gloucester was one of the many English customs adopted by William the Conqueror. Edward the Confessor had spent Easter at Winchester, Whitsun at Westminster, and Christmas at Gloucester. This tradition, although it was not kept up from the early 1100s, was maintained in the early years of Williams reign. The crown wearing was also the occasion of a Council. At Gloucester, at Christmas 1085, the king 'had much thought and very deep discussion about this country – how it was occupied or with what sort of people . . . and had a record made . . . what or how

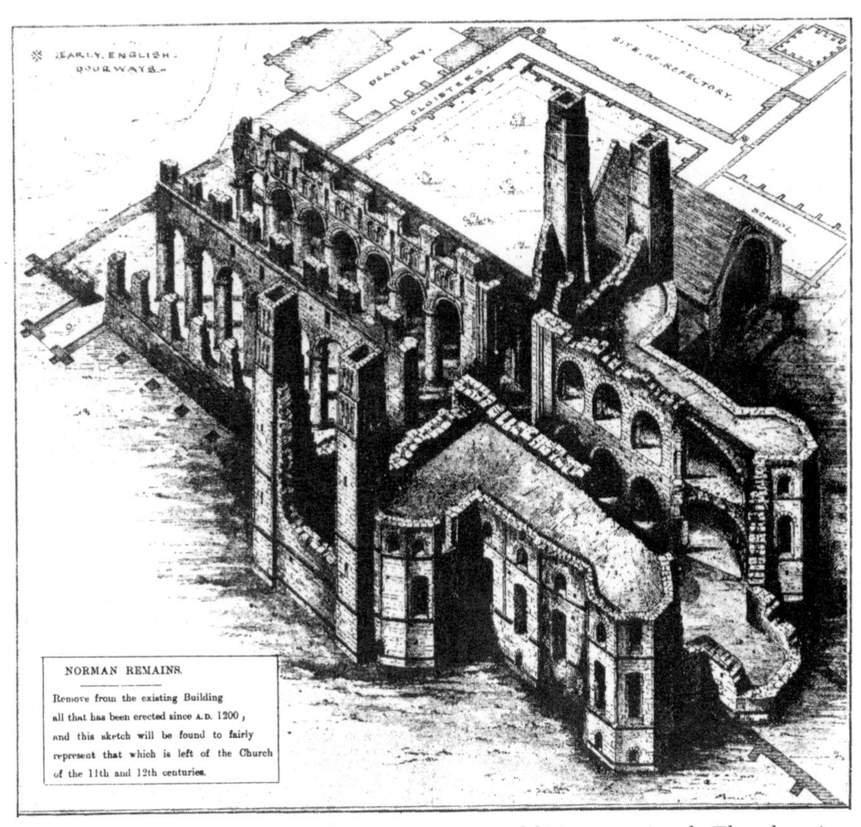

Gloucester Cathedral, with all post-Norman additions omitted. The drawing shows how much of the present building dates to the late 11th and early 12th centuries. The drawing was made by Waller, Cathedral Architect in the late 1800s.

much everybody had who was occupying land in England, in land or cattle, and how much money it was worth'. So the decision was taken to compile Domesday Book. It is often asked in which building that decision was taken. The most likely place for the Council would have been the royal palace of Edward the Confessor's time, which as we have seen had been well-accustomed to large numbers of visitors back in the 1050s. The Saxon hall would have been the setting for the Council's decision, just as it was the Saxon hundredal system of local government which enabled the Domesday Commissioners to carry out their immense task.

The nave of Gloucester Cathedral, showing the cylindrical columns of Serlo's church, begun 1089, and dedicated 1100, although the nave was not finished for several decades after that. *Courtauld Institute of Art.*

William the Conqueror at a feast before the battle of Hastings: a similar scene may be imagined when the order was made for Domesday Book to be compiled.

Another famous royal visit took place after the Christmas of 1093, when William Rufus, having been taken gravely ill at Alveston, was taken to Gloucester, perhaps to the Kingsholm palace. He was believed to be dying. He had not been popular with the church, having appropriated many ecclesiastical revenues, but on this occasion, in fear and remorse, Rufus bestowed estates on Gloucester Abbey and elsewhere. This was also the occasion when Rufus insisted on the saintly monk Anselm accepting the Archbishopric of Canterbury. Rufus was to regret his fit of munificence, and according to the Chronicle, on his recovery, took back what he had given. In fact, in the case of Gloucester, some at least of the Welsh estates he gave were lost again in the course of subsequent warfare.

The royal Christmas of 1093 was probably also the occasion of planning by the barons and the king of the campaign in Wales. Once again, Gloucester was a muster-point and stronghold for the subduing of the western kingdom. The conquest of Wales was a joint effort on the part of barons and Church, and the spoils of conquest were divided between the two. At this period,

The Gloucester Candlestick was commissioned by Gloucester Abbey between 1107 and 1113; it is inscribed, in Latin, 'The gentle devotion of Abbot Peter and his flock gave me to the church of St Peter at Gloucester'. The abbey must have been very wealthy to afford such an object; it is one of the great masterpieces of European Romanesque Art. *Victoria and Albert Museum.*

therefore, Gloucester Abbey acquired lands in Wales, no doubt contributing to the Abbey's increase in prosperity. This wealth was marked not only by magnificent buildings, but also in precious objects, one of which has miraculously survived. The Gloucester Candlestick, which is today in the Victoria and Albert Museum, London, was commissioned by Abbot Peter (1107–1113). It is of gilded silver, 1½ft. (500mm) high, elaborately decorated with beasts and human figures, and is one of the masterpieces of early Romanesque art. It is also an indication of the tremendous wealth the Abbey now enjoyed. The Abbey also contained riches of another kind, the relics of saints and burials of the wealthy. It is not known what relics Gloucester owned, but among those buried in the Abbey was Robert of Normandy, nicknamed 'Curthose' (Shortsocks), the eldest son of William Rufus, and inheritor of the kingdom of Normandy. In 1106 he had been defeated by his brother (later Henry I), and was thereafter kept in various prisons for 28 years. He died at Cardiff and was buried in Gloucester Abbey in 1134; a century later his memory was honoured by a coloured effigy, still to be seen today.

In the early twelfth century political power in Gloucester was in the hands of the 'Gloucester family', and their influence took physical expression in the rebuilding of the castle. Walter, son of Roger de Pîtres, and Walter's son Miles, demolished the earth-and-timber castle and replaced it, between 1110 and 1120, with a stone castle on a new site further west. The great stone keep, with associated buildings, walls, and gates, would have dominated the small timber buildings of the town; a constant reminder to the townspeople of their new overlords. It would also, of course, have been a source of prosperity, requiring labour, maintenance, and services, and creating a political and administrative centre of importance for the whole region. Nothing remains today of the old buildings, which were on the site of the County Prison, but the prison walls still enclose the castle area, and a surprising amount of the layout of the castle can be reconstructed from documentary sources.

Another major work which took place at this time was the demolition of the Roman quayside wall, which due to a shifting of the river-course to the west, was now redundant as a flood barrier or defensive line. The stones from it may have helped to build the castle, and the clearance freed land for the development of tenements, which quickly grew up all along the street.

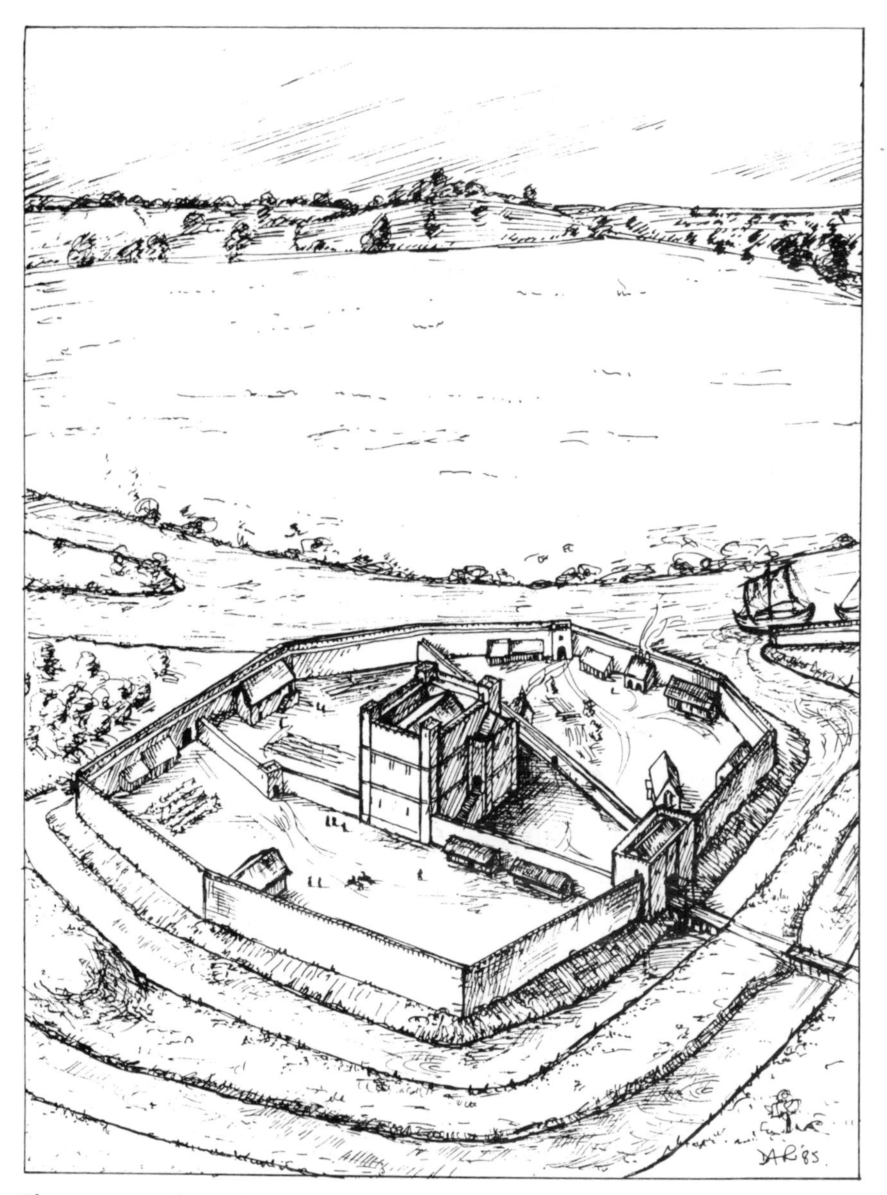

The stone castle in the late 1100s. *Drawing: Damyan Rey.*

Llanthony Prima, the abbey in the Black Mountains of Wales which was the mother-house of Llanthony-by-Gloucester. Llanthony Prima is better preserved than the Gloucester priory, which now has only the tithe barn and a few monastic buildings. Drawing in John Clarke, *Llanthony*, 1853.

This lane, now Lower Quay Street, was once the Street of the Fullers, and was known as Walkers Lane.

The castle was to be the centre of much political activity in Gloucester over the next few years. The cause was the accession of King Stephen, and the civil wars which resulted. Miles of Gloucester, Royal Constable, local Justiciar, Constable of Gloucester Castle and Sheriff of the County, was a chief actor in the saga which followed. He at first accepted Stephen as King, and in 1138 received him in Gloucester. In 1139 the Empress Maud, daughter of Henry I, landed in England, and Miles, with other great men of the kingdom, transferred his allegiance to her. In the autumn of 1139 Miles escorted Maud (or Matilda) to Gloucester, became her liege man, and from then on campaigned on her behalf. In 1141 he played some part in the battle during which King Stephen was captured; at this time the Empress was at Gloucester, and it was to Miles's castle that Stephen was first taken, although he was later transferred to Bristol. Stephen's capture meant the Empress could claim wider recognition; and so she set off for London, but she was there defeated, and was at

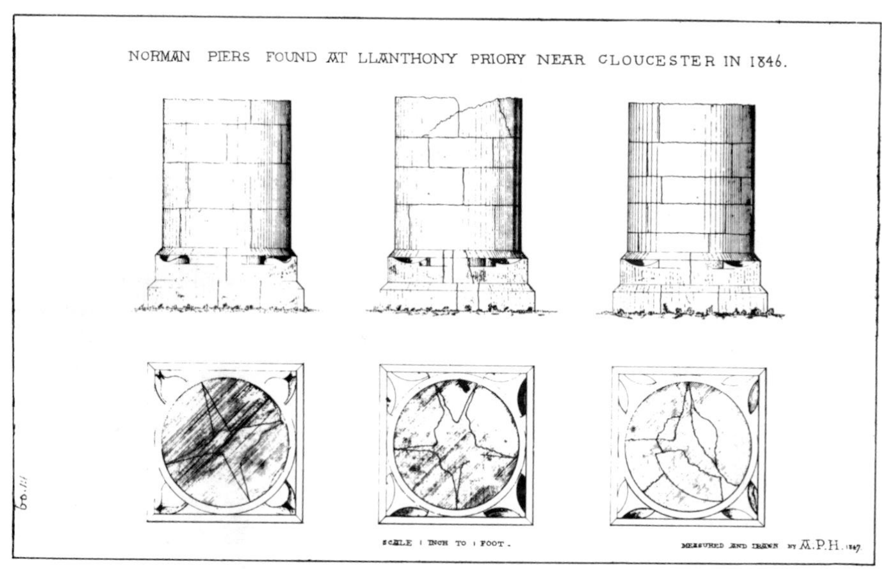

Columns, almost certainly from the priory church, found at Llanthony Priory in 1846. Each column-base is 3 ft. (300mm) square. *Glos. Coll.*

Oxford when she bestowed on Miles the Earldom of Hereford. In a subsequent campaign the Empress was again defeated and fled to Gloucester; Miles spent the next few months, the last of his life, in organising financial support for her. Miles was killed, accidentally shot in a hunting accident, in December 1143. At his death a controversy broke out over who should bury his body. The canons of Llanthony, the monastery which he had founded near Gloucester, and the Abbey of St. Peter, both claimed the honour (the precedent was important, since much future income in burial fees depended on it). Miles was eventually buried at Llanthony. His son Roger inherited his Earldom, but forfeited it by rebellion; the Earldom was suppressed in 1155, and Gloucester castle passed into the hands of the new King, Henry II.

The Priory of Llanthony, founded in 1137, reflects another aspect of Miles's warlike and intensely political existence; the urge to provide for his soul's prosperity by founding a religious house.

The origin of Llanthony-by-Gloucester lies in a monastery founded in the Black Mountains of Wales in 1108. This monastery was threatened by the Welsh wars of the early twelfth century, and the canons became fugitives, living on the hospitality of the Bishop of Hereford. Miles offered the canons land near Gloucester, and here an abbey church was built and dedicated in 1137. Miles gave the abbey much other land including the chapel of the castle at Gloucester, the chapel of St. Kyneburgh, a fishery at Quedgeley, and churches and tenements in the town of Gloucester. As Welsh conditions improved, the Bishop of Hereford tried to urge the canons to return to their Welsh church, but they could not be persuaded, and only sick or elderly monks were sent back to the house in Wales. Llanthony Secunda, or Llanthony-by-Gloucester, became one of the richest monasteries of medieval England. Today little remains of the once-splendid monastic complex; there is a fine fifteenth-century tithe barn (it is the earliest known example of the medieval use of brick in Gloucester), much-patched remnants of the great gateway, and other buildings.

Another survival of a quite different nature from the monastic period of Llanthony Secunda is its collection of records. By one of the accidents of history, there still exist eight cartularies, five registers, and a number of books from the monastic library; one of the most complete monastic archives in existence.

Meanwhile Gloucester town was growing both in size and in prosperity. Outside the north and south gates were sprawling suburbs. The northern suburb grew so large that it had in the next century to be provided with its own gate. Outside the south gate was a suburb with its own church, St. Owen, founded in 1087. To the west the town still fronted on a channel of the river Severn, and during the 1100s a bridge, named Foreign Bridge, was built over the river at this point. This bridge is now deeply buried beneath the road beside the blocks of flats known as the 'Dukeries'. Slightly later, another bridge was built; this spanned the next river channel to the west and was always known as 'Westgate Bridge'. This was built as a charitable enterprise by Nicholas Walred, a priest who may have been a member of a religious body, the 'frères pontifs', who devoted themselves to the construction of bridges. He was helped by a freeholder of Gloucester, William Myparty, who contributed a house near the bridge in which the workmen lived. When the bridge was finished, the workmen's house continued its existence as a hospital, taking care of travellers and the sick – both categories of person being, in the medieval view, equally in need of assist-

Westgate Street, 1902, looking torwards the Cross, together with the same view today. The camera is looking from where Foreign Bridge once was. The narrowing of the road towards the camera in the top picture was a relic of the approach to Foreign Bridge, which was much narrower than the road. Foreign Bridge is now deeply buried. *Glos. Coll. and C. Heighway.*

Westgate Bridge c. 1790–1800, from a drawing by Joseph Farrington. The bridge was built 1154–89 and the workers were housed in what was later St Bartholomew's Hospital. There was a gate on the bridge by the 13th century; the gate shown in this picture was built in the time of Henry VIII. *Glos. Coll.*

One of the arches of the 12th-century Westgate Bridge uncovered during road works for the new bridge in 1973. The archaeologist is Henry Hurst. *By courtesy of 'The Citizen', Gloucester.*

ance. This was the origin of St. Bartholomew's Hospital. The twelfth century bridge had a series of arches of different shapes and sizes, and a wooden drawbridge. A gate stood on the east end of the bridge by the thirteenth century; the bridge was demolished in about 1809 and replaced by a single-span structure; this in turn was demolished in 1941 and replaced by a Callender-Thompson bridge. This was then replaced by the present road bridge in 1972. The southern span of the modern bridge is approximately on the site of the medieval bridge begun in the late 1100s.

The growing town was an important centre for the production of iron nails, horseshoes, and tools; there were plenty of government orders for these in the 1100s. The cloth trade was also important, so was agricultural produce, not forgetting the Severn fisheries, which produced, among other things, lampreys (which reputedly caused the death of Henry I, and were King John's favourite food). Gloucester's quay would have seen plenty of activity, with the local craft coming and going. Where there was trade, there were also Jews, and the Jewish community in Gloucester was large enough to give its name to Eastgate Street, which was sometimes known as 'Jewry Street'. Llanthony Priory owned lands in Ireland and its canons made regular visits there to manage their property and arrange for imports of corn and other goods for the use of the Priory. Rebuilding activities were another stimulus to trade; not only was Llanthony Priory built in the 1130s, but major works were carried out at St. Oswald's Priory, which in 1150 became a house of regular Augustinian canons and at the same time enlarged its church. A leper hospital was founded outside the town. All this activity meant more prosperity for some, and wealth for a few. Some merchants became rich enough to build stone houses with a stone cellar or 'undercrofts'. Such cellars were partly below ground, both as a security measure and for cool storage of foodstuffs. One such cellar, built in the twelfth-century, is still used today – the 'Monks' Bar' of the Fleece Hotel in Westgate Street.

The ordinary people lived in timber houses, not unlike the half-timbered buildings of later centuries. Each house was set on a long narrow plot reaching back from the street frontage; most of the boundaries of these characteristic plot-shapes could still be traced in the nineteenth-century town, and many of them are still on the map today. They were designed to make maximum use of the valuable street frontage. The importance of the frontage is shown by the way the side streets of the town funnel down to meet the main street. In the back of each house-plot would be the only sanitation, an earth-dug privy; since water often came from wells dug in the near vicinity, or from the river (equally contaminated), we can assume that there were frequent epidemics of cholera and related diseases. The streets were cobbled, but infrequently, and a great deal of rubbish was flung out from houses or fell from the back of passing carts. The market was held in the main streets, so many animals being herded to and fro would mingle with the pigs and chickens kept by the householders. In Westgate Street stalls were habitually set up in the middle of the street, and gradually these evolved into more permanent shops and finally into houses. There were two

A twelfth-century undercroft; once a wealthy man's cellar, now the cellar of the Fleece, Westgate Street. *C. Heighway.*

churches in the middle of the street as well; St. Mary de Grace, at the south end of St. John's Lane, and Holy Trinity, a little further west.

Another type of religious establishment was the hospital. Medical aid was rudimentary apart from herbal remedies, but the abbeys and monasteries did their best to help severe cases. A hospital was not only for the sick; some took in travellers or were almshouses for the old or infirm. Both St. Peter's and Llanthony Abbey set up hospitals outside Gloucester; these were actually isolation hospitals for lepers (a medieval word which covered any sort of skin disease and may not always have indicated leprosy as diagnosed today). The hospitals were run by a chaplain and were under a religous rule. Today the only twelfth-century remains are the chancel of the chapel of St. Mary's Hospital, in Hillfield Gardens, London Road.

Churches and monasteries played an important part in everyone's lives. It was not only that most people were devout, but the Church in all its aspects was closely woven into the fabric of society. The three great religious houses of St. Peter, St. Oswald, and Llanthony controlled much of the life of the city. They provided alms for the needy, and schools for those who could afford the fees. They provided administrative services and guest houses for the greater folk. They owned and managed a great deal of property; half the houses in Gloucester, for instance, were owned by St. Peter's Abbey. It was usually abbots and bishops who acted as justices when the time came for the major court hearings for the shire; and the great men of the church were of course lords in their own right and had political influence. In modern parlance, the Church was Social Security, Local Government, Magistrate, and priest, all rolled into one.

There was one very important non-ecclesiastical institution; this was the merchants' guild. A guild was a trade monopoly, a 'closed shop', but it was also a social unit, composed of the wealthiest and most influential traders and merchants. These men were also freemen or 'burgesses', and they were a vital influence in the government and growing independence of the town. The burgesses had many privileges: they had trading advantages of various sorts, and had rights in the common pasture around the town. They alone were admitted to the guild. Later there were many guilds, one for each trade, as well as small guilds that were simply associations for social or religious purposes, but the guild of merchants was the most important and claimed to represent all the important men of the town. These men were beginning to desire independence for their town, mainly because it was in their financial interest to negotiate their own returns and handle their own revenues. Gloucester's first charter, in the middle years of the century, was granted by Henry II and involved only fairly limited privileges, freedom from tolls and certain court procedures: the revenues were still controlled and collected by the royal sheriff.

Between 1165 and 1176, the town's dues to the king were paid separately from those of the rest of the county, as though some measure of financial independence had been achieved; but the burgesses lost ground when they were fined in 1170 for attemp-

An 11th-century wood-lined well found during archaeological excavations outside the South Gate. It shows there was already a suburb here. As elsewhere in Gloucester, the water supply depended entirely on such easily-contaminated sources. *Western Archaeological Trust.*

ting more independence than approved of by the royal authority. Under Richard I the burgesses were finally granted 'the farm of the borough' and King John in 1200 confirmed the grant and increased the privileges of the burgesses. John's charter specifically mentioned the merchants guild, showing that it was the agency by which the town, or rather the more influential members of it, acted collectively.

The charter of 1200 provided that the burgesses should elect two reeves, or bailiffs as they were later called, and four coroners (an office which carried much wider duties than it does today). Financial management of the town was from then on dealt with by the bailiffs with the help and consent of the burgesses. The bailiffs collected revenues and presided over the local court; out of the town's income they had to pay the annual fee to the Crown, maintain roads, bridges, and defences, and occasionally

St Mary's hospital (Hillfield Gardens, London Road) was founded c. 1150 for lepers. The top picture shows the hospital chapel before its nave was demolished in 1861. Below: the chapel today. *Glos. Coll. and C. Heighway.*

undertake extra burdens, such as providing supplies for royal visits, or for the army, or helping to maintain the castle. Though Gloucester was still a part of the shire, and therefore under the control of the County Sheriff, it now had control of its own revenues. It was not always to be an easy task.

NORMAN GLOUCESTER: WHAT TO SEE

Gloucester Cathedral, Chapter House, Treasury, and Crypt (Guides available, April to October: Crypt open only at certain times).

- Cellar of 'The Fleece', Westgate Street (known as the 'Monks' Bar').

- Tower of St. Mary de Lode church, outside West Gate of Cathedral.

- St. Nicholas Church, Westgate Street; part of nave has round Norman columns: note also Norman south doorway with tympanum.

- St. Mary Magdalene, Wotton Pitch (in Hillfield Gardens, west side of London Road, about a quarter of a mile outside city centre): Norman chancel (the nave was demolished in 1861) of the 12th-century leper hospital.

- St. Mary's Gate, in the Abbey precinct: interior has Transitional Norman vaulting.

- Tables set, and other late 11th-century objects and pottery: Gloucester City Museum.

- St. Mary de Crypt church: north doorway (restored).

- Remains of Norman East Gate; viewing chamber under Boots, Eastgate Street.

- St. Oswald's Priory; arcade of arches c.1150.

Walls and Wars: The Thirteenth Century

Murage Account: money paid to Robert of Honsum and John de la Hay. For quarrying stone and paying for six boat-loads and carrying it to the Severn – 36s. For carrying the said stone from Elmore – 24s. . . . For buying lime – 18s. For a pound of lead – 36s. For one digging tool known as a 'matock' – 12d. . . . For hire of men . . . for one day 20s 2d.

Thus in 1298 one of the Gloucester stewards wrote his record of expenditure on the city walls and bridges. It happens to be the earliest account which has survived, but there were many others throughout the thirteenth century. Maintaining the walls and gates was one of the headaches for those who managed the city; they had to organise the repairs and raise the money to pay for them. The defences could not be neglected. Gloucester was still a military strongpoint of importance, and the king Henry III and his son Edward, often embroiled in power-struggles with the barons, needed the defences of Gloucester to be kept in good order. One way of financing the defences was to ask the king to grant the town the right to levy a toll called 'mureage' on goods coming for sale in the town. This was the principal source of income for wall-building, and the Gloucester bailiffs levied the tax and accounted for its expenditure throughout the 1200s and into the 1300s. In the 1200s, therefore, Gloucester's defences were transformed. The East Gate had two enormous drum towers built onto it; between the towers was a gateway with doors and a portcullis. Along the east and south side of the Roman walls were constructed a series of semi-circular bastions. In the north-east corner of the Roman wall was inserted a small gate known as the Almesham Postern. The limit of the northern suburbs outside the Roman walls was now marked by a new Outer North Gate, flanked by two small square towers, three storeys high. The site of this gate is under the Inner Relief Road, where it crosses Northgate Street. On the road north to Worcester was Alvin Gate;

The 13th-century East Gate: a reconstruction of its appearance in the 17th century. In the 13th century there was a wooden drawbridge in front of the gate. *Drawing: Richard Bryant.*

the name is Anglo-Saxon, and the gate may be earlier than its first mention in the late 1100s. Alvin Gate and the Outer North Gate marked town limits, but no line of defence ran between them, showing that they were principally toll barriers, marking the point where dues had to be paid. Near St. Oswald's Priory was the Blind Gate. There was a gate on the new West Bridge. Each gate had a porter, who lived over or near the gate; his job was to close the gates at night, preventing the entrance of

The East Gate exposed in excavations in 1974. *Gloucester Museum Excavation Unit.*

undesirables. He also had to collect tolls (or annual subscriptions) from those bringing in produce for sale, and he occasionally had civic duties as well. All Gloucester's gates were demolished in the eighteenth century or before, but the medieval East Gate has been recovered by archaeological excavation, and it can be seen today. Much of the town wall was still Roman, patched and refurbished. Outside the walls was a ditch, in which flowed a stream of water known (on the north) as the Fullbrook. Beyond these gates and walls lay the fields and hedgerows; beyond today's bus station and railway station, and east of the Library and Museum, the countryside began. The Park, today 10 minutes walk from the city centre, was once part of this farmland, which fed and enclosed the town.

Meanwhile, as work on the defences continued, the castle, the King's responsibility, was being improved and refurbished. Around the central keep were a series of courtyards with halls and chambers for the king and queen, as well as several chapels. The old palace at Kingsholm now ceased to be used for royal visits; Stephen had lodged there in 1138, and Henry III himself had been led from Kingsholm for his coronation in Gloucester

The foundations of one of the semi-circular bastions added to the city wall in the 13th century, excavated in 1969. *Gloucester Museum Excavation Unit.*

Cathedral in 1216 (crowned, it was said, with his mother's bracelet). From this time onwards, the old Saxon hall fell into disuse, and the castle took its place as the king's stronghold and occasional private residence.

Castle and town became embroiled in the baron's war of 1263–4, and were occasionally even at war with one another. The troubles were recorded in dialect verse by Robert of Gloucester, a monk of St. Peter's Abbey and an eye-witness of the events. In 1263, possession of the castle was in dispute between king and barons. Roger de Clifford and John Giffard, for the barons, besieged the castle and captured it, but Roger de Clifford then changed sides and declared for the king. The town until now had been closed against the barons, but John Giffard and John de Balun entered the West Gate disguised as woolmongers. Once in, the two barons flung off their cloaks, showing that they were fully armed, and the terrified porters handed over the keys. The barons brought in an army across the bridges and occupied the town but failed to take the castle. Prince Edward made an abortive attack on the West Gate, then took over a ship which was on its way to Tewkesbury (it happened to belong to the Abbot of Gloucester) and gained access to the castle by water. There followed bitter fighting between castle and town resulting in a royalist victory. Edward was a vindictive man. The unfortunate porters who had let in the 'woolmongers' were hung from the West Gate, and Edward imprisoned the burgesses in the castle 'as thieves and traitors . . . without mete and drinke', releasing them on payments of a large ransom. Edward then 'destroyed all the town'.

Later in the year Simon de Montfort, Henry de Montfort, and Humphrey de Bohun Earl of Hereford, with the King and Prince Edward as prisoners, spent fourteen days fortifying the town and castle. Edward later escaped, and rejoined his followers; they approached Gloucester from the north, and were able to enter the town by scaling the Abbey wall into the orchard; they then drove the garrison into the castle. Grimbauld Pauncefoot, for the barons, raised the drawbridge and defended the castle, but surrendered three weeks later. Not long afterwards, Simon de Montfort was killed at the battle of Evesham.

Edward's 'destruction' of the town has not left much trace, and there does not seem to have been a drastic fall in its moderate prosperity, although for a time some landlords claimed difficulty in collecting rents.

Scenes from the Barons' War: from a sculpture by David Gillespie Associates on Boots Store, Eastgate Street. *Bill Meadows.*

In the meantime a new religious movement was spreading rapidly through Europe. The friars became popular in England in the early years of the thirteenth century. The principal aim of the various orders of friars was preaching and teaching, particularly to the poor, in contrast to the old Benedictine orders which were secluded from the world. The friars also dedicated themselves to poverty – another attribute not conspicuous amongst the monks, who had by now amassed great wealth. The Dominican order, or Black Friars, came to Gloucester in about 1239. They were given a site in the centre of Gloucester which had once been occupied by the old castle; Henry III gave the friars gifts of timber to construct their church. The friars' churches were large spaces,

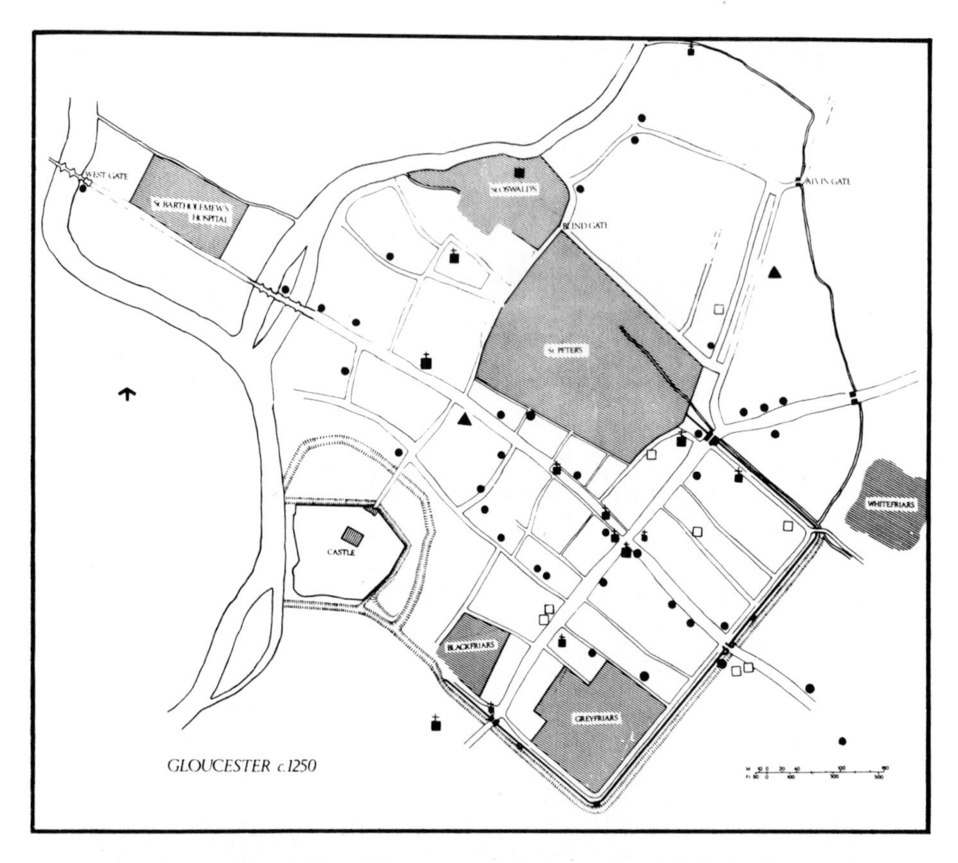

Map of Gloucester in the 13th century: the round symbols indicate where pottery has been found and so shows where people were living: the square symbols with crosses are churches. Hollow square symbols show where stone houses stood, as mentioned in documents. The tone indicates the large areas of the town which are now occupied by the various religious houses. To the north is a suburb, outside the city wall, which has its own gates, Alvin Gate and the Outer North Gate. The inner (eastern) channel of the river flows past St Oswands Priory, where there may have been a quay. This channel later silted up: today it is not visible at all.

The inside of the 12th-century church of the Blackfriars, showing the original scissor-braced roof. In the 16th century the church was converted by Sir Thomas Bell into a grand house known as 'Bell's Place'. *Bill Meadows.*

intended for preaching to large congregations, and their design was simple, in accordance with the friars' spurning of ostentation and riches. Gloucester has one of the finest surviving examples of a Dominican friary church of the thirteenth century. It is remarkable both for its simplicity and its conservatism: it still used the round 'Norman' column which had gone out of fashion elsewhere. The two ends of the church were chopped off when it was converted into a house in the sixteenth century, so that sixteenth-century fireplaces hang oddly on the church walls. But the dimensions of the preaching space still impress, and the church retains its original scissor-braced roof. Two hundred trees were used to build the roofs of all the buildings at Blackfriars; many of the oaks came from the Forest of Dean, but some from Gillingham (Dorset), and the way the oaks were cut shows that the friars used every possible piece – they never knew when the king would decide to send the next consignment. Blackfriars is remarkable not only for its medieval roof but also in being the most complete example of a Dominican house in Europe, for not only the church but most of the friars' buildings survive. The terraced houses in Ladybellgate Street hide the west range of the cloister, the friars' dining room or 'refectory'. The south range too still stands, with its original floor and roof; this was the friars' dormitory, and it also contains a row of study cubicles, each with a window, where the friars sat at their books.

Another friars' house was that of the Grey Friars. The church ruin which is visible today is an early sixteenth-century building, reconstructed by the Berkeley family only decades before the order was suppressed at the Dissolution. A third friary was that of the Carmelites, founded in the 1260s; this was a more

Blackfriars friary; the south range. The original roof and floor survive. These windows lit the friars' study cubicles.

'The Reliquary', a screen in Gloucester Cathedral dating to c. 1230–1240 which may once have formed the entrance to the 13th century Lady Chapel. *Courtauld Institute of Art.*

secluded order and it occupied a space outside the walls of the town which had been open fields. Nothing remains of the White Friars church and buildings; its site is underneath the Bus Station.

While the friars were having great success with their mission and attracting crowds to their churches, the older establishments were not neglected. St. Peter's Abbey continued its unceasing rebuilding programme. This was the period when the new Gothic architecture was coming into fashion, a style known as 'Early English'. A new Lady Chapel was built east of the choir – nothing survives of this chapel now, but a screen which may have marked the entrance can still be seen. A spire, also now superceded, was built in 1222. In 1242 the new vault over the nave was finished, and this has survived. Part also survives of the great Infirmary, the hall where monks who were ill were cared for and kept apart from the rest of the monastery. Nearby, under Little Cloister House, are thirteenth-century cellars and

The 13th-century door in Miller's Green leading to the cellars which were used in monastic times as storage rooms.

from the outside can be seen a doorway of the same date which leads down into them.

At St. Oswald's Priory the north aisle was extended and enlarged, the nave extended to the west by two bays, and new cloisters and refectory built. The two pointed arches with their foliate capitals, at the west end of the ruin, remain of the church extension. At the lower end of Westgate Street, St. Nicholas' church also has thirteenth-century work; the south aisle, with its oddly archaic round-headed windows, was added to the church in the 1200s, although the tracery in these windows is Victorian and they have been heavily restored. Similar restoration has taken place in the thirteenth-century chancel of St. Mary de Lode, and on the thirteenth-century exterior of the Abbey's West Gate, St. Mary's Gate.

Meanwhile the traders and inhabitants of Gloucester continued to live in wooden houses crowded close together. The town was inevitably prone to fire and in the early part of the century there was a series of fires, culminating in 1223, when the

A 13th-century cellar under 74–76 Westgate Street. The building above looks 20th century, but it has a 15th century roof. *National Monuments Record.*

whole parish of St. Mary de Lode burnt. Another disaster was recorded in 1300, when wooden houses in the great court of the abbey caught fire, 'but people came running from all sides, with much shouting, and the fire was quickly put out'. Not all fires were so easily dealt with. In the 1200s the authorities attempted to ban the use of thatch as roofing material, but it is unlikely that many people could afford to use ceramic roof tiles, and these did not come into common use for some centuries. Wooden tiles, shingles, were probably used. With the town densely packed with wooden houses, a stone building meant protection from fire, so some wealthy men would construct stone cellars for storage and safe keeping. One of these survives today under a store in Westgate Street. Occasionally a rich merchant could afford a stone house. Tanners Hall, between Worcester Street and Hare Lane, probably started life as a merchants house; it was a fine stone building with a hall and entrance on the upper floor. It survived until the early part of this century, when it was converted into a garage. Now only a fragment of wall remains.

Within the walls and new gates, with here and there soaring

John Clarke's drawing, published 1863, of Tanners' Hall, east of Hare Lane. This was originally a late 13th-century merchants house with a hall on the upper floor, reached by an outside stair. It was used for centuries as the Tanners' Guildhall. It survived until the early 19th century (below) when it was mostly demolished. *Glos. Coll.*

buildings in the new Gothic style, the life of Gloucester continued. Parliament assembled in Gloucester in 1278; the king's mint continued to operate. The moneyers were substantial men; four of them held office as bailiff. The town had many other important industries: iron-working and bell-founding, cloth-making, leather-working; there were glovers, girdlers, soapmakers, glasswrights, goldsmiths, hoopers, needlemakers, and many more.

Among these hundreds of traders and craftsmen there was one group of people never mentioned in any of the records. These were the poor, those on little or no income who lived by casual labour, begging and crime. They may have been as numerous or more so than the employed, and their numbers would increase in times of recession and bad harvests, as people came into the towns in the hope of better things. It was these people who were hardest hit in difficult times, who died in the fields in the severe winter of 1257–8. It was amongst these people that the crime rate was highest; amongst them would be found the petty thieves and pickpockets who were brought before the borough courts. Often there were more serious crimes. Gloucester, we must remember, was a dangerous place. There was no police force. The town was divided into four wards, each under the jurisdiction of one of the bailiffs, who was responsible for bringing cases in the borough court; but it was expected that arrests be made by the citizens themselves, by raising the hue and cry if necessary. The town streets were narrow and totally unlit after dark. God-fearing people shut themselves in their houses at dusk, but even so thieves might break in, kill everyone in the house, and escape with any valuables. This was more likely to happen in the suburban areas, which were unprotected by walls, gates, and porters; but even within the walls crimes of violence were not uncommon; for every man carried a knife, and everyone drank ale, often to excess.

A window on thirteenth-century crime is provided by the court records of the justices who came to Gloucester in 1221 to hold the assize court. Due to the anarchy of John's reign it had been seven years since the last court was held: in that time in Gloucestershire there had been 250 cases of muder. Twenty-four had taken place in Gloucester and its suburbs, where there had also been two cases of rape. This murder rate was very high: it perhaps represents one in every 1500 of the population per year, and is more than fifty times higher than the rate in 1984.

Above: St Bartholomew's Hospital was founded in the early 12th century. Its chapel was rebuilt in the 13th century and was recorded by Samuel Lysons before being destroyed in the rebuilding of the late 1800s. *Glos. Coll.*
Below: detail of a 13th century column from St Bartholomew's chapel, uncovered by archaeologists during road widening in 1972. *Gloucester Museum Excavation Unit.*

The jury which heard the cases was unlike a modern one in that the twelve men from each hundred were witnesses as well as jurors: they told what they knew, the judges pronounced sentence. There was of course no police force to apprehend or detect the criminal and in many cases the jurors simply did not know who had carried out the crime. If there was a suspect, he had nearly always run away, in which case nothing could be done but outlaw him. The men of each hundred were held responsible for any amongst them who had committed crimes: if the suspect could not be produced, the community was fined. If the accused could be produced, his evidence was heard before the jury, who gave their opinion as to his innocence or guilt. A century before, trial would have been by ordeal or by battle; now the beginning of a trial in the modern sense could be seen, but there was no doubt that any suspect, even if innocent, was safer escaping into exile. If a man was caught in a serious crime, robbery, murder, or arson, he would be imprisoned by the bailiffs until the next court (which might be years away): however men of any substance could usually purchase bail; indeed the jurors complained that the sheriff had arrested innocent men so as to collect their bail money. The under-bailiffs, or serjeants, kept the town prison, probably one or more of the city gates. These were damp and disease-ridden, and likely to cause the death of anyone unlucky enough to be incarcerated in them. However, the gaols were easy to break out of (or else bribery had its place here too). In case after case, where a suspect had been imprisoned, the jurors went on to say that he had subsequently escaped.

The judges at the court of 1221 were Randolf, Abbot of Evesham, Simon, Abbot of Reading, and the famous lawyer Martin Pateshull. They heard a very miscellanous collection of cases; anything, in fact, which was held to concern the royal interest. The jury of Gloucester said, for instance, that Robert of Aqua had found two lead coffiins full of bones (they were probably Roman): it was decided that the coffins were to be given to one of the leper hospitals. Simon the Tanner had killed Walter Bailey: Simon fled, and Henry and Adam, who were witnesses, fled too. Adam was captured and locked in gaol, but escaped and took sanctuary in St. Peter's church, and then escaped to Ireland. Simon, Henry and Adam were outlawed and their possessions were confiscated by the Sheriff who declared they were worth 6.5 marks, 22d, and 0.5 marks respectively. In another case, robbers came by night to the house of Edith, a widow, and killed her, her son, and four other people. The sheriff, Engelard of Cigogne, arrested three neighbours, and demanded bail from them. The jurors said that these three had been innocent. Later another man, Edmund, ran away; he was therefore suspected of the murder: he was a vagrant who had no possessions. The hundred was fined for not being able to produce the murderer. The jurors dealt with accidental death as well: a surprising number of people had fallen from horses and been drowned in the Severn. As for the possessions which had been confiscated by the sheriff, he was supposed to hand over the money to the king, but Engelard, a favourite of John's, managed to avoid paying up, on the grounds that he had been involved in a lot of expense in fortifying castles for John. John's favourites had clearly profited from their sheriffdoms, and it was not surprising that the town bailiffs and burgesses of Gloucester were eager if possible to gain independence of the King's Sheriff. This level of self-government was not achieved until 1483.

THIRTEENTH CENTURY: WHAT TO SEE

- East Gate, 13th-century city gate, and exhibition showing other 13th-century defences.

- Blackfriars church: the remainder of the monastic buildings are not yet open to the public.

- Cathedral: the screen ('Reliquary') in the north transept; vault over nave; infirmary hall (ruined arches to north-east of cloister); door of cellar outside Little Cloister House; cellars of Little Cloister House (can be visited by prior arrangement).

- St. Oswald's Priory: west end of nave.

- St. Nicholas' church: south aisle (restored).

- St. Mary de Lode church: chancel (restored).

- St. Mary's Gate, entrance into Abbey Precinct from the west: exterior (restored).

- Chapel of St. Margaret's Hospital, London Road (opposite Hillfield Gardens).

The End of The Middle Ages: The Fourteenth and Fifteenth Centuries

For a brief period in 1321–2 the town was again the centre of political squabbles between the King and the barons; the Mortimer party occupied the castle and town. The King's victory resulted in the hanging at Gloucester of the leader of the baron's party, John Giffard. From this time onwards, however, Gloucester was tending more and more to take a backstage role on the national scene, as its military importance decreased in significance. The population of Gloucester was around three or four thousand and it ranked fifteenth in the tax assessments; it was a moderately prosperous town a little larger than Hereford and about a third the size of Bristol.

1348 was the year of the great plague, the 'Black Death'. The Gloucester authorities ordered that no travellers to or from Bristol should enter the town. Many people actually left for the safer air of the countryside; the city bailiffs ordered that they should be fined for every day of absence. It was obvious that if too many people of consequence made their escape there would be nobody to manage the town at all. Precautions were in vain; the sickness reached Gloucester some time in 1349. At Llanthony Priory, nineteen out of the thirty canons died, and this may be an indication of the death-rate in the city. If half of the population did die, then the loss was soon made up, probably by immigration from the countryside.

Gloucester, throughout the 1300s and 1400s, gained its living from two principal manufactures: cloth and iron goods. It also benefitted from its weekly market, its annual fair (granted to the city in 1301), and its visitors. These might be merchants, or customers for the markets, but occasionally there were arrivals of more consequence, as the King or even the King and his Parliament, made the journey to Gloucester. Parliament met in Gloucester in 1378, 1407, and 1420. The Parliament of 1378 was held in a building in the Abbey precinct; the stone foundation of

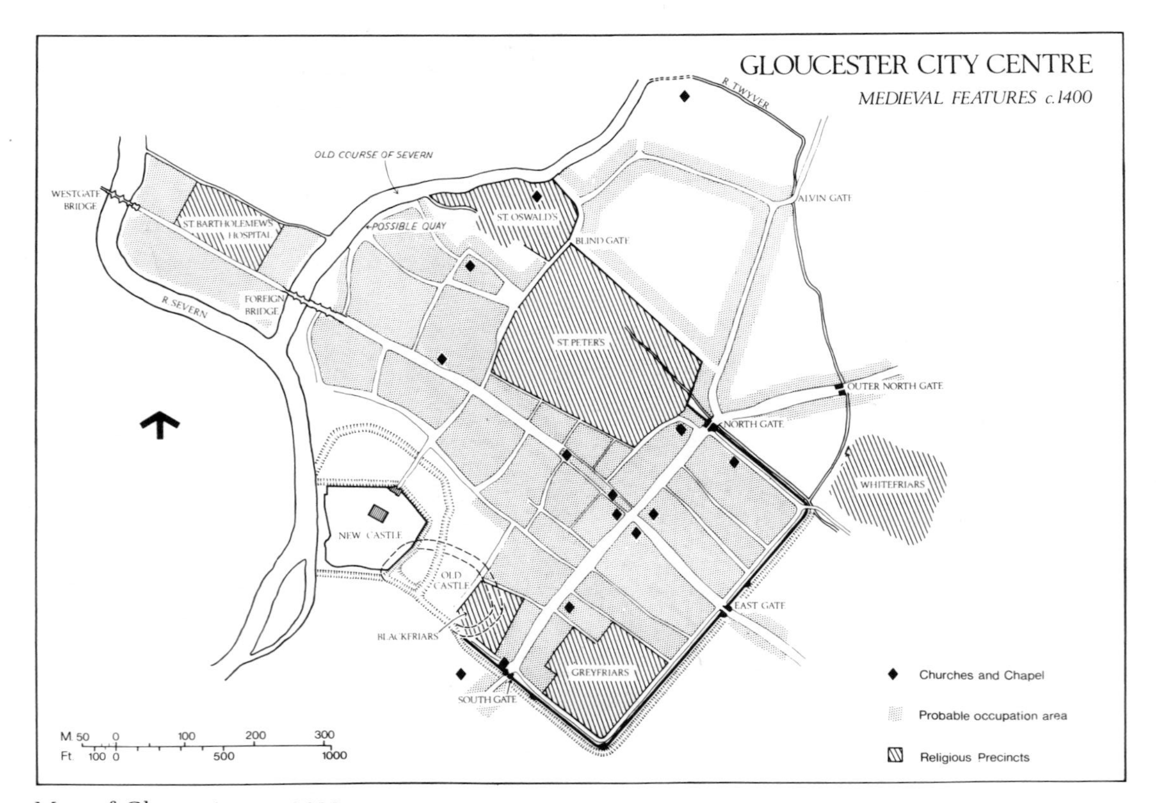

Map of Gloucester, c. 1400.

Detail of the tomb of Edward II in Gloucester Cathedral. Edward's murder in 1327 made him a martyr, and pilgrims to the tomb increased the abbey's revenues. *Courtauld Institute of Art.*

this 'Parliament Room' can still be seen today, although there is a fifteenth-century building on the older walls.

There were pilgrims too. These increased in number after the murder of Edward II in Berkeley Castle in 1327. Edward had not been popular in his lifetime, and his supporters were not doing well at his death. Yet after his murder he began to be revered as a martyr and saint. His body, buried at Gloucester Abbey, became

The choir of Gloucester Cathedral: the basic Norman structure is masked by the Perpendicular work begun after 1337. *Courtauld Institute of Art.*

The cloisters of Gloucester abbey, built in the late 14th century. In the south walk, shown here, is a recess with a stone trough, the monks' washing-place. *Courtauld Institute of Art.*

a focus of pilgrimage and therefore a source of income for the Abbey, and the new king, Edward III, made further donations in his father's memory. There were other sources of income too for the Abbey, for it had great estates on the Cotswolds and elsewhere, and had a good share of rising profits resulting from the high price of wool.

Throughout the fourteenth and fifteenth centuries Abbey buildings were repaired or replaced. A new dormitory was built in 1303–13. In 1318 the south aisle of the nave had to be rebuilt; the windows were decorated with ballflower ornament. During the reign of Edward III the great south window was created; it is the earlest extant Perpendicular window in the country. The soaring Perpendicular lines of the remodelled choir were com-

The tower of the abbey, completed in about 1470, and still a landmark to the surrounding countryside. *By courtesy of 'The Citizen', Gloucester.*

plete by the mid 1300s, and the rebuilding of the cloisters was finished by 1400. The west end of the nave, and the west front, were rebuilt in the early 1400s. The tower was finished by about 1457, and the Lady Chapel, the final glory of the fifteenth century, was complete in 1499. The Abbey was not responsible only for ecclesiastical buildings; within the Abbey precinct there had to be housing for guests and for workers and medieval buildings of this date still survive. The Abbey also indulged in speculative building, and had several inns built so that it might profit from the increased tourist trade. One of these, the New Inn, was built and named shortly before 1455, and is still trading today.

Gloucester continued to have many trades and industries. By now many crafts had their own guild, or trade association, which controlled entry to the trade by regulating apprenticeships. Each guild had its own chapel in one of the churches, and many, though at first meeting in private houses, later had meeting halls of their own. The merchants guild, the most important of all, had its hall, the Booth Hall in Westgate Street. One of the most important guilds was that of the tanners, who worked in the northern area of the town, many of them in Hare Lane, then known as Tanner's Street. They had a chapel in St. John's church, and rented for their hall the upper room of a stone merchant's house which became known as Tanner's Hall. Of all the guilds, those concerned with the wool and cloth trades were the most important: the biggest craft guilds in 1400 were the weavers, fullers, and dyers. Those engaged in the more elegant aspects of the cloth trade, merchants in the drapery or clothing line, were the leading men in the town. Gloucester's other main source of income, the iron trade, is commemorated today by the street name of Longsmith Street, and also Broadsmith Street (now Berkeley Street); in the 1300s and 1400s these lanes would have rung with the sound of hammers. When archaeologists dig up houses which stood in these streets, they find workshops and forges with thick layers of hammer-scale and smithing slag, the accumulated waste from years of working iron. A great number of specilialist trades related to iron manufacture also went on in the area, where one could find cutlers, bladesmiths, coopers, farriers, and pinners. All made their goods and sold their wares in the shops and workshops in the centre of the town. Northgate Street and Eastgate Street were much quieter areas, where professional people lived; the craftsmen here were glovers and weavers. Those who did not manufacture for the retail trade lived further out of the town: the tanners outside the north gates or at the extreme west end of the town. The butchers and mercers were all congregated at the higher end of Westgate Street. Among the merchants were the Whittingtons, who leased a house next to St. Nicholas Church. Richard Whittington did indeed become Lord Mayor of London and marry Alice FitzWilliam, although his origins were anything but poor.

A few wealthy men made their living from overseas trade with the Continent and Ireland. Seagoing ships seldom reached Gloucester, however; the stretch of river below the town was treacherous and difficult and the cargoes were transferred to smaller craft at Bristol. These foreign imports were wine, salt fish, and Baltic timber, while the return trade was in cloth and corn. Corn, grown in the fertile Severn Valley, was an important element in Gloucester's down-river trade from the 1300s onwards. Gloucester was also important for the internal trade with its hinterland, but river trade never made a substantial contribution to its fortunes. Towns further up-river, Tewkesbury and Bewdley, were fierce competitors with Gloucester, and there was a good deal of dispute with them about trading rights and river tolls. The cross-river trade with Wales was considerable, which meant that the maintenance of the bridges and causeway was vital. An important product from Wales was cattle, both for meat and for hides for Gloucester's leather industry. Another commodity that came in through the west gate was of course iron, carried on packhorses from the Forest of Dean.

Gloucester's market sold agricultural produce from an area around the town of about six miles. Traders brought in bread, ale, honey, fish (especially salmon and lamprey). Gloucester housewives could have bought a variety of jugs and cooking pots made locally, some brought in by river from Worcester and Bristol. There would always, of course, be imports of the raw materials for all the trades, bales of wool, hides, oak-bark, and dye for the tanners. The most vital commodity was salt; without it food could not be preserved for the winter. The market would also have sold luxury goods brought in by the merchants from Bristol and London. To transport some of these goods packmen and carriers would be necessary, and some men were engaged in the haulage trade. Travel by road was always difficult and dangerous: indeed it was a medieval charity to aid travellers and contribute to the repair of bridges; hence the roadside chapels on

A 15th-century pottery jug.

main roads, where people could pray for a safe journey and also contribute to the upkeep of the road. In Gloucester, St. Bartholomew's hospital next to Westgate Bridge was an example of a bridge chapel which helped with its revenues to maintain the safety of Gloucester's link to the west.

All this incoming traffic, wagons, carts, animals too, was crowded into the narrow streets in which the markets were held.

The Cross in the centre of Gloucester, c. 1730: a watercolour by Paul Braddon. The painting, though dating to 1730, shows the centre of the town much as it would have looked in the 15th century. Behind the cross on the left is the Tolsey or Council House: on the right the buildings which occupied the centre of Westgate Street. On the extreme left are shops built against St Michael's church. *Arlington Mill Museum, Bibury.*

The Kings Board; a preaching pulpit and butter market which stood in the centre of Westgate Street and is now in Hillfield Gardens, London Road. *C. Heighway.*

There were other obstacles in the streets. Stone crosses, for instance, were set up at several points. The most famous was at the central point of the town, which is still known as 'the Cross' even though the stone cross was demolished more than two hundred years ago. In the middle of Westgate Street was 'the King's Board', originally a preaching pulpit, but also used for the sale of butter and cheese. The stocks and the pillory also stood in Southgate Street, where offenders condemned by the local court were exposed to the derision of the by-passers.

The cobbled streets, as in former centuries, were resurfaced only occasionally. In the fourteenth and fifteenth centuries the bailiffs were allowed to levy a tax called 'paveage' on goods coming into the town, but this was never enough to keep the streets in reasonable condition, and they were deep in mud and filth of every kind. The bailiffs issued orders that each householder was to keep clean the street in front of his house, but this order had to be repeated so often that it is quite clear that the system did not work. The butchers in particular were forbidden to throw their offal into the street, and householders were frequently told that their pigs and ducks must not be allowed to wander.

Fresh water was always a problem. It was recognised that it was unhealthy to tip sewage into water-courses, but still many people had wells in their backyards which could be all too close to the privy. The major abbeys and friaries had had a piped water supply for some years. From 1438 the water supply of Greyfriars was 'borrowed' by the city which purchased the right to tap the Friary's water supply, brought in lead pipes from Robinswood Hill. It now fed a public conduit at the High Cross, and provided the only supply of fresh water for several thousand people and a considerable number of industries.

Houses were still of timber, built of wooden frames with wattle and daub infill, with storeys overhanging the street. Not many houses of this date have survived in Gloucester. The most famous is the New Inn; with its two courtyards, external stairs, and decorated timbers. Other fine examples of timber-framed houses are in the Cathedral Close.

From the main trading street, Westgate Street, there were two narrow lanes leading to gates in the Abbey wall. St. Michael's Gate was the entrance by which funeral processions passed to the lay cemetery. The lane was known as 'Craft Lane' or Ironmonger Row. The other lane (now called College Street and

The New Inn, built by Gloucester Abbey before 1455. *Bill Meadows.*

widened) led to King Edwards Gate; its medieval name was Lich Lane. Beyond these gates was the large walled area of the Abbey Precinct, and within those walls was a whole world separate from the town, and yet closely connected with it. The most important person in this busy complex was the abbot himself. He was supervisor of the monastic life and a man of devotion and learning, but also, the medieval paradox again, a man of rank who attended court, entertained royalty, owned country houses and a house in London, and even kept hunting dogs (perhaps for the use of his guests). The Abbot, through his deputy the Prior, was responsible for the monastery's main purpose, prayer and worship, but the abbey's properties, and its duties to the poor and sick, meant much other work, such as collecting rents, keeping business records, drawing up leases, organising help for the poor, teaching in the monastic school, supervising rebuilding both inside and outside the abbey, seeing to the welfare of guests, in fact a whole complex of management tasks.

Alongside all this activity was the rigour and quiet of the monastic day. The monks rose at 2 a.m. and filed into the church for the first services of the day. There followed a continuous pattern of services and duties until Compline, the last service of the day at dusk. The duties of some monks would include work in the vineyard or herb garden, copying books or studying. There was a wide range of different monastic officials, such as the precentor, who cared for the music and music books, the cellarer, who was the abbey's quartermaster and estate manager, and the kitchener, responsible for meals. The infirmarian cared for those monks who were sick, and he was in charge of the monks' hospital or infirmary. The almoner gave money, food and clothing to the poor.

Today it is possible to see many of the monastic buildings and to recapture something of the life of the monastery in the last years before its dissolution. Most visitors enter by St. Edward's gate: this is sixteenth-century, and has only the west tower surviving, but a gate existed here in the twelfth century. The line of the abbey wall, through which the gate passed, and the east tower of the gate, are marked out in the road. On each side of College Street are garage entrances: these are the built-over remnants of a medieval lane which once ran all the way round the abbey walls. College Green is the Outer Court of the Abbey. It is surrounded by houses which look eighteenth-century, but which conceal some earlier buildings, converted from monastic structures. No.8, College Green, is a fifteenth-century timber-framed house with a restored facade. College Green can also be entered by St. Mary's Gate from the west. Beside the gate is the Almoners Lodging: the half-timbering is sixteenth-century, but the earlier stone foundation still shows the window where the dole was distributed. On the north side of College Green, near the west front of the abbey church, stands 'Church House'. Its main front is Victorian Gothic, but this conceals an immensely complex building dating to the twelfth century, when it was the Abbot's Lodging.

On the north side of College Green an arched entrance leads to 'Miller's Green', the Abbey's catering area, where the abbey mill stood, also the kitchen, buttery, and larder. Under the ground are several stone-lined watercourses which brought fresh water for washing and cooking and to drive the mill. One of these stone watercourses fed a stone cistern which can be seen in the central garden of the Great Cloister. In Miller's Green is the fine late

The 'Parliament Room', a late 15th-century hall on 13th-century stone foundations. Richard II's parliament of 1378 was held here. *Bill Meadows.*

fifteenth-century timbered hall of the 'Parliament Room'. A building of similar date, with an original window, can be seen between Nos. 4 and 5. On an upper floor above No. 2 was the monks 'misericord', where they were allowed to eat meat if they were ill. Beyond is the Little Cloister, a secluded small garden in Perpendicular style, where the infirmerer would grow his herbs, and the sick monks could rest. Nearby is the infirmary itself. But the glory of the monastic precinct is the Great Cloister, with its study cubicles on the south side. The monks were not allowed to talk here, but could, if they wished, communicate with visitors in the West Slype. Above the East Slype (Treasury) is the monastic library, built in the fourteenth century. It retains much of its original roof.

The Abbey, with all its activity and power, was not the only organisation of its kind: there were, for instance, the two houses of Augustinian canons, St. Oswald's and Llanthony. The Au-

The 14th-century gateway of Llanthony Priory: a print c. 1800 published by Samuel Lysons. The left-hand portion of the main arch has now gone. *Glos. Coll.*

The 14th- or 15th-century tithe barn of Llanthony Priory. The cores of the walls are of brick. Llanthony was enormously wealthy. Its property included land in Gloucester, and some of the richest farmland in Ireland. *C. Heighway.*

gustinian canons also lived under a Rule, but it was less strict than the Benedictine one, and all the canons were priests who looked after the parishes under their jurisdiction and cared for the poor and sick in the way expected of medieval monasteries. Llanthony Priory was flourishing in the fourteenth century and was able to build the great tithe barn which can still be seen; one of its canons also acted as Renter for the city and the priory, and kept the records of property owners and their arrears. Among the Llanthony records are several rent rolls, one of which, for 1455, has been published: it is a valuable source for the fifteenth-century town. Its careful entries, recording each householder, the previous holders, and the rents due, provide a fine example of the organisational ability of the monks and canons, whose skills they often rented out to local lords or to the city authorities. Llanthony also kept the city school, although it was often in dispute with St. Oswald's Priory over which establishment had the sole rights of the school. Llanthony also had a magnificent library: a catalogue of the books which it owned in about 1300 gives 486 original entries: by 1380 there were over 530 volumes, an unusually large number.

Considerable as their skills were, the monks and canons no longer had a monoply of learning, nor were they now the only recipients of people's generosity. In the fourteenth and fifteenth centuries the universities at Oxford and Cambridge were taking over intellectual leadership, and gifts to the monasteries were dwindling. Wealthy people were much more inclined to leave their wealth either to their parish church, or to endow a chantry (a priest or group of priests who would say masses for the person's soul after their death).

The town itself may have been suffering a decline in prosperity in the 1400s, although it is difficult to be sure since the bailiffs tended to exaggerate their difficulties in order to reduce the amount due to the King. In 1487 the burgesses complained to the King that houses were in ruins, that there were only 300 dwellings left in the town; and that money was needed to repair the walls, gates, and bridges 'which brugge, wallis, yatis and towres be now very ruynouse, and have great need of reparacion, and like to fall in desolacion . . .'.

In the meantime Gloucester had made an important advance in its long struggle for independence. It had been granted, in 1483, a charter by Richard III. This charter changed the constitution of the towns government; instead of the four bailiffs there was now

Bronze closing-ring from St Nicholas church: early 14th century. *Gloucester City Museum.*

to be a Mayor, aldermen, and a common council on the London model. The status of the town also changed: it became a county in its own right, and took into government a large part of the surrounding countryside (the 'inshire'). Richard III also remitted the fee due from the town, and did not (as was usual) charge it a sum of money for the privileges contained in the charter. With reduced liabilities, extended area and income, and a new constitution, the town was set to enter into the new century with improved prospects.

FOURTEENTH AND FIFTEENTH CENTURIES: WHAT TO SEE

- The Cathedral: Effigy of Edward II, *c*.1330; South aisle, 1331–5; Great south window in south transept, *c*.1335; Choir 1337–51, and choir stalls, *c*.1350; West end of nave and west front, 1421–37; Tower, *c*.1450; Lady chapel, 1500.

- Cathedral precincts: Great cloister, 1351–1400; Little Cloister; 4–5 Miller's Green, timbered 15th-century house; Parliament Room and Laud Room, late 15th-century.

- New Inn, Northgate Street, 15th-century.

- King's Board, Hillfield Gardens, London Road, late 14th-century

- Llanthony Priory, Tithe barn and gateway, 14th-15th century

- St. Michael's Tower, at the Cross, 1465 (Tourist Information Centre).

- St. Nicholas, Westgate Street; tower.

- St. Mary de Crypt, Southgate Street, 1461–1501; also late 15th-century wall paintings.

- City Museum, Brunswick Road: Closing ring from St. Nicholas' church, 14th-century. Pottery, 14th-century.

- St. John's Church, Northgate Street: tower.

- 99–101 Westgate Street (Folk Museum): late 15th-century.

Privatisation and Puritans: The Sixteenth Century

First and foremost rode alle the burgesses in array ii and ii; next them the skarlett gownes; then alle gentilmen, esquyers, knyghtes, lordes, and other great men; and then the Maire opyn hedde . . . and the Kyng of Arrodes with hym; then rode next the Kyng he that bare the swirde, and on every side of hym a sergeaunt at armys with ther masys. And then folowid the Kynges grace and the Quene, with all the lades and gentilwomen followyng them . . . bryngyng His Grace into the Abbey throwght Seynt Edwardes Lane, the Abbot and his bretherne, then beyng in the Abbey Churche porche with coopys, crosse, carpettes, and cusshynges, receyvng His Grace.

Thus, with great ceremony, King Henry VIII and his Queen entered Gloucester in 1535. In his ride through the town the king had paused outside Whitefriars, and then entered Gloucester through the north gate. He would have been able to view, perhaps with an avaricious eye, several of Gloucester's monasteries and friaries. He was to begin their dissolution in the following year, and the process was complete by 1540.

The new Tudor monarchy was aggressively nationalistic and could not tolerate religious groups which held allegiance to a foreign power, namely the Pope: Henry VIII was now himself Head of the Church. The monasteries had accepted Henry's supremacy, and those under foreign control had been suppressed in the previous century. Henry's suppresion of the remaining monasteries was the end of a long process. By now the monasteries were in decline. The numbers of monks or friars were few, and many monasteries were in financial difficulties. St. Oswald's, at its dissolution in 1536, had seven canons and eight servants, and it was in debt. The church was ruinous, although the living quarters were in good condition. By the time the

St Michaels Gate; one of the entrances to the Abbey; rebuilt in the 16th century. The 'Tailor of Gloucester's' shop occupies a space which was once a lane which skirted the abbey wall. *Bill Meadows.*

Remains of the 16th-century Bishops' Palace in Pitt Street. When the diocese of Gloucester was formed after the Dissolution, a palace was needed for the new Bishop of Gloucester. *C. Heighway.*

Friaries went to the Crown in 1538, many of the friars had already fled abroad. By then Blackfriars only had a Prior and six friars, Greyfriars five and the Carmelites three. Llanthony, dissolved in 1539, had already by 1481 dwindled to the prior and four canons. The great Abbey itself was surrendered last of them all in 1540. The Dissolution, although it heralded the start of a religous reformation, was not in itself a reform, but only a change of ownership. A scramble followed to buy up the properties of the monastic corporations, which in many cases passed into lay hands. At Gloucester Abbey, the old order was preserved, for Henry VIII created a new diocese with St. Peter's Abbey church as its Cathedral, now served, for the first time since 1022, by a college of secular canons (hence the names College Street, and College Green). The Cathedral inherited most of the Abbey property, ensuring continuity of many aspects, both good and bad, of the medieval system, and providing jobs for many of the dispossessed monks.

Since there were few surviving friars and monks, it was not difficult to provide for them. Some received pensions: the old Prior of St. Oswald's was given £15 a year. Many friars or monks became parish clergy. Some with influence did much better: the ex-abbot of Tewkesbury, for instance, became the new Bishop of Gloucester. The new Dean was John Jenyns, a favourite of the King's who was also able to buy up most of the property of St. Oswald's. Many parish churches, with their property, continued to be managed as before, with the owner (either Cathedral or lay person) collecting the income and providing a stipend for a curate. Churches continued to be invested in as real estate, often in plurality, and often to the detriment of their parishioners, for some curates were so badly paid that only poor and ignorant men could be persuaded to take on the job.

Another institution which continued much as before was the bishop's court or consistory court. Once this was presided over by the Bishop of Worcester or his chancellor: now such a court was also held in Gloucester. These courts tried cases of moral misdemeanor such as adultery or incest, or religious backsliding such as failure to attend Communion.

Much monastic property passed into the hands of any well-to-do men of the town who were able to invest in it. Some of the new owners seem to have been aware that they had also taken on the charitable obligations of the monasteries: they were public benefactors as well as landowners. A good example is Thomas Bell. He purchased Blackfriars church and all its buildings, as well as a great deal of monastic property in the city. He converted Blackfriars into a house for himself, demolishing both ends of the church and inserting floors and windows. The friars' dining hall and other domestic buildings were converted into a cloth manufactory for the making of caps and probably for other cloth-making activities as well. Thomas Bell was said to have

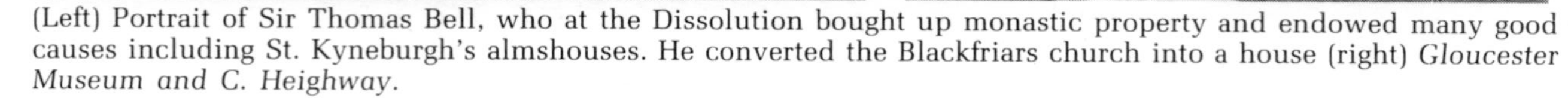

(Left) Portrait of Sir Thomas Bell, who at the Dissolution bought up monastic property and endowed many good causes including St. Kyneburgh's almshouses. He converted the Blackfriars church into a house (right) *Gloucester Museum and C. Heighway.*

St. Kyneburgh's hospital; almshouses built by Sir Thomas Bell. *Glos. Coll.*

employed some 300 men, a number which almost merits the description of a 'factory'. Thomas Bell also built an almshouse beside the site of the old Saxon chapel of St. Kyneburgh near the South Gate: this was for six poor folk; part of the old chapel was retained for the use of the inmates of the hospital. He also had other property in the city which was used for the maintenance of poor people, and he left in his will (he died in 1566) money for the poor and for prisoners in local gaols, as well as for the maintenance of the two west bridges. He was an important man in Gloucester, being an alderman and becoming three times Mayor. He was knighted in 1546. The name of his wife is commemorated in the name 'Lady Bell's Gate'; there was once a gate to the friary in Ladybellgate Street, although it was there long before Lady Bell's time.

Another benefactor in the same mould was Joan Cooke. Her husband John died in 1528, leaving her a wealthy widow. John Cook had been one of the town's first aldermen, and served several times both as Sheriff and Mayor. At his death he made

The Crypt School, next to St Mary de Crypt church, endowed out of monastic property by John and Joan Bell in the 16th century. *C. Heighway.*

many bequests to the town, including money for the upkeep of highways and roads (very much in the medieval tradition), for the repairing of St. Bartholamew's Hospital, and for the poor generally. Most important of all were the bequests of his wife Joan, who was carrying out her dead husband's wishes when at the dissolution she purchased a large part of the estate of Llanthony Priory and used it to endow the Crypt School next to St. Mary de Cyrpt church in Southgate Street. Thus education in the city continued to be provided for. Such education, it need hardly be said, was for the sons of burgesses and tradesmen. Women rarely received any regular education, and the children of the poor almost never.

Another Gloucester benefactor was Richard Pate. This man had actually been a commissioner under Henry VIII and had helped to survey the religious houses before their dissolution. He was thus in a good position to assess the property, much of

Priory House, converted out of the west monastic range of St Oswald's Priory at the Dissolution. It was demolished in 1823–4. Top picture: the rear of the house, from 'Gloucester from the North-West' by William Marlow (1740–1813) *Gloucester City Museum*. Below: the front of the house from a drawing by J.C. Buckler, c. 1819. *Bodleian Library, Oxford*.

The church of the Greyfriars, rebuilt by the Berkeley family in the early 16th century not long before the Dissolution. Its east end is under the new market. *C. Heighway.*

which he was able to purchase. Some of his wealth was used to endow a grammar school at Cheltenham. He lived in Gloucester and was an influential man in the sixteenth century, several times representing Gloucester in Parliament.

The fate of the monastic buildings in Gloucester was various. St. Oswald's Priory had been exceptional in having its own parish. The parishioners had been accustomed to worship in the north chapel of the church. By 1538 the whole building was in bad repair, and it was adapted by demolishing the nave and converting the north aisle into a church, with the north transept becoming the chancel. The Tudor doors and windows which were inserted to block the openings of the north aisle, are still visible. The west range of the cloister was converted into a large mansion, called Priory House, which was to survive until the nineteenth century. Llanthony Priory fell into ruins and was badly damaged during the siege of Gloucester. The church of the Grey Friars was purchased by a brewer, who converted it into a manufactury for ale: it was later converted to a row of shops, as the ruins of today still show. The church and buildings of the

Carmelites seem to have been converted to barns and outhouses: they too suffered during the siege, and did not survive after that time. The Abbey of St. Peter became the Cathedral church, but some buildings such as the monks dormitory and refectory, were demolished.

The end of the monastic establishments did not mean that England automatically became Protestant. Henry VIII, having declared himself head of the church, still remained a Catholic in all but the matter of papal supremacy. The Protestant movement was growing, but there was widespread attachment to the old religion. In Gloucester Thomas Bell was one of those who were bitterly opposed to the new ideas: he was said to be responsible for the dismissal of Hugh Rawlings, parish priest at Holy Trinity, Gloucester, on the grounds of negligence. There was a Reform party as well, which wrote to Bishop Latimer to complain of Bell and his friends. It was clear that the town was deeply divided over religious issues, and the differences were made sharper by the appointment of Bishop Hooper to Gloucester in 1550.

Hooper was a reformer who had spent some of his youth in Switzerland where he had acquired Lutheran ideas and a Protestant wife. There was considerable opposition to Hooper's appointment from the bench of Bishops, and Hooper at first refused to take up his appointment because he objected to wearing the rich vestments, which he regarded as 'Popish'. After being committed to the Fleet prison, he was persuaded to change his mind, as long as the vestments would only be worn occasionally for ceremonial purposes. He entered into his duties in 1551. He began by carrying out a visitation of all his clergy, which showed that more than half were unable to repeat the ten commandments, and some were even ignorant of the Lord's Prayer. Their ignorance was at least partly a result of the poverty of the allowance made to them, often in turn due to the fact that the income of the church was appropriated to some landowner. Hooper was powerless to correct this medieval system, which was to survive for years, but he did attempt to improve the stipends of some of the poorer clergy. He also undertook his other duties conscientiously: unlike his predecessor, he presided himself in the consistory court and imposed penances rather than fines. He also preached two or three times a day, and provided dinners for the poor in his palace. It was probably Hooper and his adherents who were responsible for removing or defacing statues of saints in the Cathedral, and taking away

Bishop Hooper, burned to death in Gloucester for his Protestant faith. A 19th-century monument stands on the place of his martyrdom. *Gloucester City Museum.*

wooden screens in other churches of the diocese. He was not Bishop for long, for in 1553 Queen Mary ascended the throne, and began her attempt to eradicate the Protestant movement by force. Hooper was tried for treason and sentenced to death. In 1555 he was brought to Gloucester and lodged in Lower Westgate Street, traditionally in the building which now houses the Folk Museum. He was burnt in St. Mary's Square, on the spot where his statue now stands. His death was horribly prolonged, for the wood was damp and the fire had to be relit twice. The onlookers were deeply impressed by the bravery with which he met his death.

The creation of martyrs hampered rather than furthered Mary's cause. Most of them were not men of rank, as Hooper had been, but workmen of one sort or another: ten people were burned in all in Bristol and Gloucestershire in Mary's reign: two of these were executed at Gloucester, apart from Hooper; they were Thomas Drowry, a 'blind boy', and Thomas Croker, a bricklayer. There were many other people who recanted of their Protestant ideas, but even so Protestants were probably a minority. Queen Elizabeth, when she ascended the throne, still presided over a country which was only midly Protestant, and she intended to keep it that way. Extreme Protestantism, or Puritanism, was a threat; it created disaffection among ordinary people and questioned the power of the state. Roman Catholics had been declared traitors, but dealing with Protestants was more difficult. Elizabeth's middle view was imposed in Gloucester by the Consistory Court, which was ineffective, and later by the local sittings of the Ecclesiastical Commission.

Sessions of the Ecclesiastical Commissioners began in Gloucester in 1574. Elizabeth was herself visiting Gloucester that year, probably a significant coincidence. This was the bishop's Consistory Court with added teeth, for the judges were empowered, as never before, to use civil penalties such as imprisonment to force conformity. To aid the Commissioners, civil persons of local importance sat among the judges, men such as the Mayor and Sheriffs of Gloucester. The court inquired into every aspect of life, whether moral or religious, both of clergy and of layfolk. We might today see this as an infringement of personal liberty, but the Commissioners were concerned with the stability of the realm. Moreover, the Commission's efforts, though much fiercer than the consistory courts, were not always successful.

The clergy who appeared before the Commission were most frequently accused of unsuitable behaviour, and of not maintaining the chancels or parsonages for which they were responsible: thus Roger Grene, rector of Stratton, 'could not excuse himself to be often-times overcome with drinke and the parsonage house in great decaye'. Other clergy were accused of unsatisfactory morals, or of popish practices. Some of the cases heard by the Commissioners had been dragging on in the Consistory Court for years; in most of these the Commissioners quickly resolved the problem, in some cases by dismissing the incumbent.

Of the lay persons interviewed by the Commissioners, only

one was accused of papist practices, and in this case the defendent had been spreading propaganda. It was as though the commissioners were anxious not to stir up too much the latent conservatism of ordinary people. The Puritans were a different matter. Their offences included not taking Communion, or refusing to go to church; they claimed they objected to the observing of Holy Days, or the clerical wearing of surplices; they also refused to have their children christened, denouncing baptism as superstition. William Drewitt and his wife refused to have their child christened, in spite of spells in prison, finally vowing that if the child was forcibly christened 'they wolde never receave yt againe nor take yt for their chylde any more'. Joan Pride, in July 1575, was so incensed by the 'papism' of her local cleric that she shouted at the court that 'yt were a good deede to sett dogges on the minister to hunte him out of the church'. In nearly all these cases the Commissioners had in the end to admit defeat, in spite of terms of imprisonment, excommunication, or long and earnest lecturing on the part of the Commissioners themselves, who were prepared to argue for hours to persuade the Puritans of the error of their ways. In the end the Commissioners only increased the resentment felt by Puritans towards the high and local commissioners, a resentment which was to end in Puritan victory and the abolition of the commissioners' courts by the Long Parliament of 1641.

The Consistory Courts, however, continued: indeed they still exist today. One of the reasons they fell into such disrepute in Gloucester in the late 1500s was due to the Chancellor, Thomas Powell. The Chancellor presided over the courts in place of the bishop: it was unusual for the bishop himself to take on the business, as Hooper had done. Chancellor Powell conducted the Gloucester Consistory Court for nearly twenty years from 1559. He was notoriously corrupt. It had become usual by then for public penance to be commuted for a money payment: Chancellor Powell found it convenient to pocket the payment himself. When the defendant was rich, Powell extorted more. He issued illegal marriage licences, for a fee, and, while he sat in judgement on the morals of others, lived himself a notoriously licentious life. The incredible thing was that the bishop, clergy, and indeed most ordinary people, were well aware of Powell's activities, yet no-one dared to disturb the social order by bringing charges against him. In the end, a quite minor quarrel with the Cathedral clergy in 1578 led to charges being made, that he 'hath bine of longetime, and yet is, a fornicator, and adulterer with many wemen and maydes, and a committer of rape . . . a common haunter of tavernes, a drunkerd, a blasphemous swearer'. He was often incapable of conducting the court, especially in the afternoon; he had 'committed riots' in the Cathedral churchyard, failed to administer justice, and had not received communion for four or five years. He was dismissed, but his long rule had brought the bishop's court into considerable disrepute so that it was known to Gloucester people as 'the bawdy courte'.

The Roman Catholic campaign to win back converts in England touched on Gloucester a few years later. Thomas Alfield of Gloucester had visited the Roman Catholic training seminary in Douai in 1576, and later smuggled Catholic books into the country, enlisting into the cause Thomas Webley, of Gloucester. Alfield and Webley were executed at Tyburn in 1583. Two Roman Catholic priests were executed in Gloucester in 1586 or 1587, as well as a Gloucester glover, excecuted in 1588.

Gloucester, a city now that it had a cathedral, achieved even greater status in 1580, when by decree of Elizabeth the town was made a port. This meant that it had control of a wide customs area, and was able to increase its revenues. Bristol complained bitterly, but to little effect; in fact her trade was probably little affected. Gloucester's port books now recorded a lively trade with Worcester, Bridgnorth, and other river ports. Gloucester was in dire need of extra revenues, for in the 1580s the war in Flanders depressed trade in general. Furthermore, the decline in the cloth industry and related trades such as clothing and cap-making, created an increase amongst the unemployed. Poor harvests, high grain prices, and frequent plague epidemics also increased the city's difficulties, and swelled the numbers of the poor and destitute.

Everyday life for the employed in Gloucester was a long working day at crafts and trades. Fewer people now worked as clothiers and weavers, but there were plenty of leather workers, and the tanners still carried on their trade. By far the largest proportion of people were involved in the retail trade: mercers held nearly a quarter of the common council seats between 1580 and 1600. From their large shops near the Cross mercers and haberdashers sold luxury or semi-luxury wares to gentry and well-to-do farmers from the countryside. Some of the goods had been imported via Bristol like the quantities of oranges, wines,

St. Nicholas' House, now the 'Dick Whittington'; a fine 16th century house with an 18th-century addition on the Westgate Street frontage. *C. Heighway.*

oils, and raisins listed in 1583; others, like the latest fashions in dress, came from London.

Amongst the reasonably well-off people who worked in Gloucester a surprisingly high number of men, about half, could write, although only about 4% of women could do so. Basic literacy was taught, for a fee, in the dozen or so local schools: these were the ordinary man's counterpart to the gentry's schools, the Crypt Grammar School and the Cathedral school.

A high proportion of the people living in the city would have been in service, and have come from outside the city; wages were low and even the poorer households could pay a servant. An average household would have consisted of a couple and children and one or two servants, all living and working together as a unit. It is a myth that medieval families consisted of large numbers of relatives all living together; it was common for a couple to set up business and house on their own, and in any case the high death rate usually meant that extended families were unnecessary. Late age of marriage (on average 23 or so for women; 25 for men), meant that fewer children were born. The infant mortality rate was high too, though not so great as used to be thought: perhaps between a fifth or a sixth of infants died in their first year. The average size of the majority of households, including servants, was in fact about five. These families lived in timber-framed houses, or a few rooms in such houses. Few ordinary houses of this time have survived in Gloucester today: the ones which can be seen were the best-built, the houses of the rich, such as St. Nicholas' house (now the 'Dick Whittington'. Other buildings were added to Gloucester's landscape in the sixteenth century: a new gateway was constructed on Westgate Bridge in the time of Henry VIII, and a Customs House was built on the quay in 1581. The streets were still very dirty; regular street cleaning was in the future and it was left to the householders to clean the streets in front of their own house – never a successful enterprise. The problem of loose livestock was still current and in 1572–3 one of the city stewards recorded in his accounts 'paid for twoe peaces of timber for to make a pounde for the shriveffs to putt in the pigges that goethe about the citie xvs [15 shillings]'. There were many inns and alehouses which were also a source of worry to the city authorities, because they might shelter trouble-makers and also women of ill-repute: hostellers were told not to harbour any person more than three days 'without perfect knowledge what they be' and were also forbid-

The late 16th-century Booth Hall, Westgate Street, replaced in 1816 by the present Shire Hall. From *Illustrated London News*, January 1847; *Glos. Coll.*

den to keep 'common quenes ore strompettes'. The inns were also meeting-places for forbidden games, as gambling with dice or cards.

Crime was as much of a problem as ever. Public punishment or imprisonment were the consequences. There was a 'scolding cart' in which quarrelsome women were driven about the city; the stocks and pillory continued to be used, being renewed in the middle of the century. There was a ducking stool as well. Thieves were branded on the hand. Prisoners were held in the city gates; the castle was the county prison; offending burgesses, however, were kept locked in the Booth Hall, where they were certainly more comfortable than in the gaols. The gaolers were miserably paid, and had to augment their incomes by charging prisoners for the unpleasant accommodation they occupied.

'Robert Raikes' House' in Southgate Street in the 19th century. It is little changed since the 16th century, except for the ground floor, which has been altered, although with old timbers. *Glos. Coll.*

The poor were a severe problem for the city authorities. Since the early 1500s the aldermen attempted to limit the number of beggars by licencing a certain number and providing them with badges and livery. The number of poor increased and was especially high in the 1590s: beadles (policemen) were employed who whipped unlicenced beggars out of town. Attempts were made to find useful work for the poor, and in the late 1500s a House of Correction or Bridewell was created. For a time at least this was in the 'New Bear' next to the Booth Hall in Westgate Street. Bridewells originated as workhouses: shelter and food was provided in return for work, the idea being that the poor be made to support themselves. In the early 1600s the beadle received a bonus for every beggar he arrested and sent to the Bridewell. The work done there included various manufac-

St. Margaret's Hospital, in London Road. In the 13th century it was a leper hospital, but in the 16th it was re-established as almshouses. The almshouses were demolished when London Road was widened; the 13th-century chapel in the foreground still survives. *Glos. Coll.*

turing schemes, the most common being pin manufacture. In the early 1600s the Bridewell was moved to the East Gate, where the poor worked on weaving and pin-making. The city authorities also attempted to stockpile grain and coal for the use of the poor. All this effort on the part of the aldermen was not just Puritan conscience for the wellbeing of the poor; there was also an element of fear of dissaffection and riots, as the number of poor became greater and the rich richer but fewer. During 1586 clothworkers rioted in the city over shipments of grain out of Gloucester at a time of acute shortage: there was more disorder in 1604 at the height of a plague epidemic.

Outbreaks of plague occurred every few years and were severe in Gloucester's crowded and poverty-stricken tenements. Special isolation-houses were set up; for instance outside the wall near the East Gate where there was garden ground but few houses. Deaths from plague, which in the parish of St. Nicholas at least, were one tenth of the population in the epidemic of 1603–5, were not as severe as in the larger towns such as Bristol, where a quarter of the people died. Gloucester was able to make up its population, by immigration and natural replacement.

Help for the poor was also provided through the reorganisation of the city hospitals and almshouses. These had not been wound up at the Dissolution but had been taken over by lay persons. St.

Bartholamew's was reorganised and extended in 1569, and in the 1590s the city took over St. Mary Magdalen's hospital. Later, in the 1630s, all the hospitals came under the control of the aldermen. It was, however, typical of the time that places in the almshouses were reserved for impoverished freeholders or their relatives. For the really poor, there was only the Bridewell.

Poor relief and the other necessary measures for running the town cost the authorities a great deal. In the early 1550s the four stewards were still balancing the books with a slight surplus, but from the 1560s the deficits mounted each year. The trouble was that the income, from rents and tolls, remained the same, whilst prices continued to rise. By the 1570s the city could only stay solvent if each incoming steward took on the deficit of the one before. Not surprisingly it became more difficult to find aldermen to take on the stewardships. In 1585 steward John Brooke refused to pay the debt of his predecessor and disaster was only averted by the outgoing steward taking his payment a year late.

The government of Gloucester in such circumstances tended to be in the hands of fewer and fewer men. Influence of any kind was held only by the freemen (burgesses) of whom there were about 500, and a chosen 40 amongst them who made up the Common Council. This in turn chose the men who held the real power, the Mayor and Aldermen. Councillors had mostly to take their expensive turn at serving as steward and as sheriff. Not surprisingly many councillors refused to serve, and so the aldermen tended to consist of a very exclusive group of those wealthy enough to bear this burden. The aldermen were automatically JPs, they also ran most of the guilds, governed the hospitals, and sat in Parliament.

The expense of office meant that the few who took it on hoped to make the most of it; corruption was almost inevitable. In the 1590s there was a series of frauds involving the corn-stock for the poor: Alderman Garnons was said to have profited by up to £160. Most fraud was quite minor; such matters as obtaining city leases at special low rates, selling town offices, aldermen under-assessing each other for taxes; or obtaining contracts for themselves: in 1604 plague victims were buried in civic shrouds bought from the mayor's shop. Resentment over the control by a few sometimes produced protest and agitation; it contributed to the riots of 1604. But this never became an overwhelming problem, perhaps simply because the ruling group were seen to be doing their best.

SIXTEENTH CENTURY: WHAT TO SEE

- St. Nicholas House, next to St. Nicholas Church, Westgate Street (The 'Dick Whittington'; frontage 18th-century).

- Winfield's: 26 Westgate Street: 16th-century timber-framed house with 18th-century frontage (view from passageway beside shop).

- 8 Westgate Street: room with 16th-century panelling.

- 66 Westgate Street.

- Parts of 'The Fleece', Westgate Street.

- Folk Museum, Westgate Street; relics of Bishop Hooper.

- St. Mary de Crypt Grammar School, Southgate Street.

- 36–8 Southgate Street ('Robert Raikes' House').

- Blackfriars: 16th-century house converted from Friars' church.

- Cathedral: effigy of last abbot, William Parker, *c.*1535.

- Bishop's Palace, Pitt Street: remains in Abbey wall.

- Horsepool, next to East Gate, in viewing chamber under Boots, Eastgate Street.

A City Besieged

The causes of the English Civil War and even of the resistance of Gloucester are still debated: although Peter Laslett has suggested that conflict is endemic in any society and so may need no explanation at all. Certainly for its politics to be Parliamentarian, the religious sympathies of Gloucester's ruling group must have had Puritan tendencies.

Puritanism in Glucester had grown steadily in the late 1500s, especially among the city's leaders: in the early 1600s they established a puritan lectureship, and they protested loudly in 1617 when the new Dean, high-church William Laud, replaced the altar at the east end of the Cathedral. In 1618, despite the king's recent Declaration of Sports, the maypole in St. Nicholas' parish was pulled down, it was said with the connivance of the magistrates and mayor. In the 1620s and 1630s the aldermen patronised distinguished puritan schoolmasters and tried to remodel the city hospitals on more puritan lines. To Gloucester's leaders, struggling with rising poverty and economic crisis, puritanism with its emphasis on public control and godly discipline was appropriate and appealing. In the circumstances, the demands and exactions of the Crown in the late 1620s provoked much opposition in Gloucester; so did the Crown's new religious strategy with its increase in ritual and devaluation of puritan ideals. William Laud, now Archbishop of Canterbury, opposed Gloucester's governers and had them fined for their support of John Workman, a leading puritan divine. Gloucester's economic difficulties were relevant: a city which could not feed its poor did not receive kindly the constant royal requests for money.

Before the fighting between Charles I and Parliament began, Gloucester had set up a Committee of Defence in August 1642. The seven gates were locked with iron chains between 9 p.m. and sunrise, and the keys given to the Mayor. The watch was doubled, and gunpowder, weapons, and digging tools were got

The seige of Gloucester, from a sculpture by David Gillespie Associates Ltd, Boots Store, Eastgate Street. *Bill Meadows.*

ready. Three cannon were bought. Some corporation plate was sold to get money for the defences, and loans were obtained. In December Lt. Colonel Massey arrived with an infantry regiment and two cavalry troops: he was to be the hero of the subsequent siege.

Cirencester fell to Prince Rupert in 1643 and he rode to Gloucester to demand its surrender also. Gloucester refused. The city at that stage was unprepared for a siege: fortification were unfinished and the ancient defences in a bad state. When the West Gate drawbridge was raised it fell into the river 'and was like to have drowned and spoiled several persons'. The soldiers were also mutinous, but Massey was able to impose discipline, and carried out several successful expeditions, including the capture of about 1,500 Welsh Royalist soldiers who had approached from the west. The prisoners were locked for ten days in St. Mary de Lode and Trinity churches. Then some joined the Parliamentarian cause: the rest swore not to fight again and were sent home.

In July 1643, Bristol fell to the Cavaliers, leaving Gloucester the only Parliamentarian garrison between Bristol and Lancashire. Gloucester began to prepare even more intensely for a fight. The Roman walls and gates were lined with earth, and strong 'sconces', earth bastions, were built. The City was particularly vulnerable on the north-west side, where the cathedral precinct wall and a small earthwork between the Outer North Gate and the Alvin Gate were the only defences. However, there was low-lying marshy ground in this area, and the city authorities appear to have deliberately flooded the water-meadows to impede access from north and west. The flooding must have been slight, for even during the siege cattle were led out every day across the footbridge near St. Mary de Lode church, to graze on the meadows. To the west there was no defence but the river.

In August Charles I reached Gloucester: within a few days the city was surrounded by about 30,000 Royalist troops, and on August 10th a royal proclamation was sent to the city. This offered pardon to all if they would surrender at once: their reply said that the inhabitants would 'keep this city according to our oath and allegiance. . . . and doe conceive ourselves wholly bound to obey the commands of his majesty signified by both houses of parliament, and are resolved by God's help to keep this city accordingly'. With this complicated refusal, battle began.

The Royalists might have attempted a direct assault in view of the weakness of some of the defences, but this tactic, though successful at Bristol, had been very costly in men. The Royalists therefore resolved on conventional siege warfare, which meant attacking the city from east and south, where there was good ground for siege engines and artillery.

Charles himself was quartered at Matson House, not far from the city. The defenders first burnt down all the houses in the suburbs outside the walls so as to leave no cover for the enemy. The besiegers cut the town's water pipes, and also diverted the Twyver stream so that the besieged town had to use horse mills

Civil War armour in Gloucester Folk Museum . *Gloucester City Museum.*

and drink Severn water. The Royalists dug themselves in close to the city on the south. Gloucester sent out various skirmishing parties, mostly successful in capturing prisoners and tools out of the enemy trenches. Having mounted several cannon, the Royalists began battering the walls; the defenders continued to fill the south gate with earth and to build a breast-work against the wall. Archaeologists have found a massive ditch which forms a great V-shaped bastion in front of the South gate: the ditch was full of rubbish dating to the Civil War period; pots, shoes, combs, and jews' harps.

Action on the whole was sporadic, and musketry and cannon fire achieved little. 'The enemy shot divers granadoes [a type of bomb] out of their battery into the towne; whereof about four fell upon some houses, and brake into them, but (by God's providence), did no harm, and one fell into the street near the South gate, but a woman coming by with a payle of water, threw the water thereon, and extinguished the phuse thereof, so that it did not break, but was taken up whole: it weighed 60 pounds weight.' A few days later the enemy had more cannon in position and started 'a most furious battery' on the south and east, but the earthworks stood firm. During archaeological excavations at the East Gate, a cannon ball was found wedged in a heap of stone roof-tiles just in front of the gate. This great assault killed two

The great ditch dating to the Civil War period excavated by archaeologists outside the South Gate. The scale is 2m (6ft) high: the ditch is deeper than a man's height. *Western Archaeological Trust.*

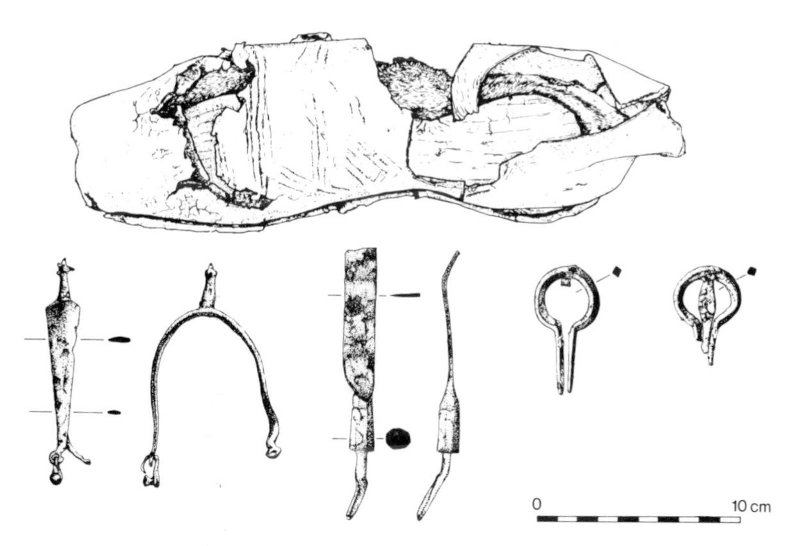

Objects dating to the mid 16th-century found in the Civil War ditch outside the South Gate: a shoe, a spur, a knife, and jews' harps. *Drawing: J. Knappe and J. Vallender; Crickley Hill Trust.*

'The South Gate, Gloucester', by R. Curzon, 1888. This gate was rebuilt after the Siege of 1643, and was demolished in the late 18th century. This picture is an imaginative reconstruction, based on other drawings. *Gloucester City Museum.*

children, and a pig, which the defending soldiers ate, with much jeering at the royalists.

Meanwhile Parliament had organised a relief force. This arrived on September 5th, having spent a night in torrential rain on Prestbury Hill. The force, led by the Earl of Essex, made its triumphant entry into Gloucester on Thursday 7th. The siege had already been lifted. It had been a close thing: the garrison had only three barrels of gunpowder left. But only 30 or 40 people had been killed, most of them shot while incautiously 'peeping' at the enemy.

The immediate aftermath of the siege involved repairing and replacing the damage to buildings. The South Gate, filled with earth and severely bombarded, had to be rebuilt 'with battlements' and new stairs added. Over the gate was set an inscription

'A city assaulted by man but saved by God' and inside another inscription read 'Ever remember the 5th of September 1643: give God the glory.' Even more expensive was the compensation of those who had lost their houses: the total damage as submitted to Parliament in 1646 was £28,720. The city was reimbursed by being given lands in Ireland, which turned out to be insufficient. Another problem was the garrison which, not surprisingly since it had never received any pay, was troublesome and inclined to desertion; the worst problems were only averted by the officers paying the men themselves. Massey himself billeted more than thirty soldiers at his own expense. Massey attempted to tax the countryside around Gloucester to raise some of the necessary money, which led to complaints from the country gentry, and a committee of officers, citizens, and country gentlemen was set up to hear complaints and see that the money was properly administered. Though this relieved Governor Massey of administrative concerns, it did not solve the problem of the soldiers' pay, which continued to be in arrears. The soldiers were guilty of many disorders in collecting horses and cattle, levying money and seizing goods without authority. The garrison was also short of supplies and ammunition. Moving supplies was hazardous: the countryside was still full of royalist troops and Massey was kept constantly busy organising counter-attacks and intelligence.

In 1645 Parliament proposed to promote Massey to be Major General of the army under Sir Thomas Fairfax. The Mayor and aldermen were alarmed: they had come to rely on Massey's ability and they did not want a new Govenor: they petitioned Parliament to leave Massey where he was. But the plea was not granted and Massey departed, much regretted. He was given a present of 'one silver and gilt bason and ewer, and two silver flagons'. Massey's successor, Colonel T. Morgan, also had severe problems in financing the garrison. In August a squabble broke out between the towns of Gloucester and Bristol over which areas each might levy tax on: the dispute came to fighting, to the alarm of the Commons, which ordered both sides back to their cities, and forbade either to levy in the disputed areas. The Commons tried to resolve the matter by making the Gloucester garrison the only one in the county; Colonel Morgan was succeeded, in 1648, by Sir William Constable, who was in charge during the traumatic year 1649 when the execution of the King took place. Sir William sat as one of the judges upon the king's trial, and signed the warrant for his execution.

By 1651 the dead king's son, Charles II, had collected another Royalist army and was fighting Parliament on his own behalf. Information that he was on his way south from Scotland caused alarm in Gloucester, where the defences were further strengthened: the Alvin Gate was blocked up with earth and breastworks built. Charles II, with an army of 12,000 men, entered Worcester on August 22nd: the Gloucester committee distributed £7 among the fourteen companies of foot in Gloucester 'for their extraordinary labour in the fortifications of this garrison for two daies and two nights past'. The Gloucester town crier made the announcements that 'all burgesses and inhabitants of Glocester, who are not listed, are to muster by themselves, servants or workmen tomorrow morning by six o'clock, with spades, shovels and mattocks and little baskets at the south gate, to work at the fortifications all that day upon pain of 5s a piece.' Meanwhile, General Cromwell's army had also assembled at Worcester, and the Gloucester accounts record that ammunition, hay, hides, and 'forty barrels of strong beere' were sent to Cromwell, including a cask of special 'double beer' for Cromwell's private use. After Cromwell's victory there was further charge on the city's accounts as a result of celebrations: including a 'quart of sack' (sherry) drunk by the mayor and 'a captain that came from Worcester' (presumably to bring the good news).

Later the same year the city elected Oliver Cromwell to be their high steward; he received, with his first fee of £5, a present of lampreys. In 1652–3 the garrison of Gloucester was disbanded, and the sconces demolished.

The Commonwealth period was one of great upheaval for the Cathedral and its clergy. From 1649 to 1660, all bishops were removed. The Bishop of Gloucester, Godfrey Goodman, was forced to flee to Wales and his houses were plundered. Most of the Cathedral Clergy lost their livings. The Cathedral revenues were taken over by Parliament, and the Cathedral itself narrowly escaped demolition. Just in time it was given to Gloucester Corporation, who declared it a parish church, and carried out urgent repairs.

In July 1657, Oliver Cromwell became Lord Protector, and the proclamation was given out at the Wheat Market in Gloucester. A platform was erected on which the mayor and aldermen sat in their robes; the proclamation was made to a fanfare of trumpets, after which wine and cakes were served for the city leaders at the Tolsey. The cathedral bells were rung, and bonfires lit. In 1658,

Richard Cromwell was proclaimed in Gloucester in the same style as his father. But Gloucester was known to be wavering in the Roundhead cause; it was at one time suggested to Charles II that Massey, who was now a Royalist, might be persuaded to capture the city and hold it for the King, which would have been a reversal of the earlier siege, and thus an important propaganda victory. This project failed, and Massey was actually taken prisoner, although he managed to escape. The city was again threatened, and had troops quartered upon it. In this precarious situation, the country went to the polls and Massey entered the city to be elected a freeman so as to be eligible to stand for one of the two city seats. An attack was made on him and there was something of a riot between his supporters and others. The incident indicates that political opinion in Gloucester was very divided. Subsequently Massey was elected as one of the city MPs, and was later knighted.

In 1660 the culmination of the political change came about, and Charles II was King. The decrees of the Commonwealth were reversed. The Cathedral clergy and bishop returned. Charles was proclaimed in the city, with great ceremony, not dissimilar to that which had attended the proclamation of the Cromwells, only a few years before. There was the usual sounding of drums and trumpets, and 'all the three conduits ran with wine for many hours'. In the evening there were fireworks. Later the Corporation sent very loyal and humble greetings to the king.

Charles II, however, had not forgotten Gloucester's earlier sympathies, and took steps to make sure the city would not oppose him again. By the Corporation Act of 1661, the town councillors, aldermen, and officers all had to take an oath of allegiance and to forswear the Puritan's Solemn League and Covenant. Gloucester's jurisdiction was reduced and it lost its surrounding lands, the 'inshire', which it had gained in 1483. Local Commissioners were appointed by the King as 'watchdogs' and these supervised the breaching of walls and the dismantling of the gates, although the defences were not, as is sometimes said, completely levelled, for they survived for many years to be used as a quarry by the city council. The Council was also purged of all its anti-Royalist members: 10 aldermen, 25 councillors (more than half) and John Dorney, the town clerk, were all removed. A new charter of 1664 specified that the Recorder and Town Clerk be subject to royal approval. This purge was not as efficient as it might have been, carried out as it was by the country gentry, who were unfamiliar with the politics of Gloucester. A dissident faction remained to create a fuss, even a riot, over the election of a royalist mayor in 1671. Robert Fielding, the leader of the dissidents, was ejected from his position as alderman, but the vote against him, 19–15, shows he was part of a substantial minority. The Crown now made greater attempts to suppress Gloucester's independence, and in a new charter of 1672 the crown reserved the right to dismiss aldermen and councillors. The council was again purged and 20 more men lost their places. The result was the intrusion into the council of many new royalist sympathisers, particularly county landowners such as the 1st Duke of Beaufort. This new Tory council gave Charles II no trouble, and followed James II in religion: from 1686–8 the town even had a Roman Catholic mayor, John Hill, who was in office at the visit of James II in 1687.

After 1688, the composition of the Council reverted to its more Presbyterian viewpoint, and the Crown ceased to dominate local political life. The influence of the country gentry remained, however. This may have been to Gloucester's advantage. The 1650s had seen a decline in social traffic as a result of Gloucester's civil war sympathies, and the purchasing power of the gentry, in acquiring goods, luxuries, visiting lawyers and surgeons, seeking entertainment, was an important contribution to Gloucester's economy. The presence of country gentry on the aldermannic bench was a help to Gloucester's fortunes.

The appearance of the town did not change greatly during the 1600s and its population increased only slightly: it was perhaps 5,000 in 1700. Some noteable new buildings had appeared; the Tolsey at the Cross was rebuilt in 1602: this was where corporation business was carried out and the Common Council held its meetings. The Tolsey was next to the church of All Saints, and in 1648 the church was converted into a court for the Sheriff. There were new courts at the Booth Hall in 1606 and a Wheat Market, in the middle of Southgate Street, constructed in the same year. In 1634 Alderman Scriven provided the money to erect a conduit in Southgate Street: Scriven's Conduit is a piece of Gloucester's past that can be seen today, somewhat incongruously placed in Hillfield Gardens. In 1655 a new Barley Market was built in Eastgate Street, making use of stone from the old church of St. Oswald's, which was ruinous. The demolition of the church was a hazardous proceeding and one of the workmen was actually paid extra for danger money. The only reason that anything at all

The conduit given to the city by Alderman Scriven in 1636; it originally stood in Southgate Street. *Bill Meadows.*

The Oak Room, Bell Hotel, dating to 1650. *Glos. Coll.*

of the Saxon church of St. Oswald survived was due to a Mr. Miles Clent, who bought the one wall which still stands today.

In 1660 the Corporation rebuilt the Market House in Southgate Street and in 1662 placed there a statue of Charles II. It was removed in the middle of the eighteenth century and was discovered in 1945 in a garden near Westbury-on-Severn. It has been re-erected in a small garden off Three Cocks Lane. The Cross was repaired and improved several times in the 1600s. There was demolition as well: the two little churches in the middle of Westgate Street, St. Mary de Grace and Holy Trinity, were pulled down. The tower of Trinity was, however, left and a conduit placed under it. A new school appeared in the late 1600s: Sir Thomas Rich's Hospital, opened in Eastgate Street in 1668. The will of the founder, Sir Thomas Rich, a wealthy London merchant, was that the school be for poor boys. It was typical of the time that the Corporation, in executing the will, decided to restrict entrance to the sons of freemen.

Wooden water pipe, preserved in Gloucester Folk Museum: part of the city's 17th-century water supply. *C. Heighway.*

These public buildings were mostly in stone, but most private houses were still built in the traditional timber. Of private buildings erected in the 1600s, there survives part of the Bell Hotel, in Southgate Street, with a Jacobean timber frontage; and 30 Westgate Street, now occupied by the Alliance Building Society. In the 1600s, this building was occupied by Mr. Comelin the apothecary, and during the siege it received a direct hit of hot shot fired from the royalist battery at Llanthony.

The Corporation's management of Gloucester's every day life began to show a little more sophistication in the 1600s. The perennial problem of fire, for instance, was met by the installation of a fire engine, which was kept in Trinity Church and was supposed to be checked by the city's Bellman to see that it was in working order. Although the streets were still filthy, it was being recognised that this was an undesirable state of affairs, and the dirty state of the streets was cited as a cause of sickness among

9 College Green, built in about 1690. *C. Heighway.*

soldiers and others during the Civil War. The inhabitants were told to clean the street in front of their houses every Saturday afternoon, and there were fines for defaulters: the beadle could impound stray pigs, and during the Civil War, if pigs were found on the defences, the soldiers were allowed to kill and eat them. Ordinances about street cleaning became more frequent in the 1650s and onwards, and 'scavengers' were appointed to take away rubbish from the streets. In 1672 the burgesses appointed one of their number as 'Common Scavenger', to be in charge of street cleaning; Mr. William Angel was paid £40 a year to undertake this duty, and the city parishes were rated in order to pay for this. Mr. Angel would have sub-contracted the work, and his post did not relieve the citizens of their duties; in the late 1600s they were still being fined for not doing their share of street cleaning. And in 1671, presage of the modern age, posts were ordered to be set up with the names of the streets upon them.

All through the 1600s Gloucester's population remained fairly static; by the end of the century there were about five thousand people living in the city and its suburbs. Something like ten percent of them would have been servants and apprentices; something like a quarter lived in poverty or near the subsistence level. The poorest parishes were those of St. Mary de Lode and St. Catherine, to the west of the town. Those who did have jobs were largely occupied in providing food, drink, clothing, and household necessities for the city and its surrounding countryside. Gloucester's clothing and textiles industry had been declining since the early 1600s, but this was compensated to some extent by the growing importance of pin manufacture: Gloucester pins were exported to all parts of the country. Other metalworking was still important, particularly the bell-foundries. The famous Rudhall family, between 1684 and 1740, cast bells for 112 parishes throughout the shire.

In spite of pins and bells, Gloucester had no early development as an industrial centre, partly because of the cramping restrictions on apprenticeships imposed by the Guilds and the Corporation. Also commercial growth was still dominated by Bristol, in spite of Gloucester's port status. Gloucester had surprisingly few people engaged in coastal trade: it had three ships in 1619, compared with Bewdley's five, Worcester's ten, or Tewkesbury's eight. The difficulty of the river passage below Gloucester was a factor here; a problem which was only to be solved more than a century later by the coming of the Gloucester and Berkeley Canal.

SEVENTEENTH CENTURY: WHAT TO SEE

- 30 Westgate Street (Alliance Building Society).
- Scriven's Conduit (Hillfield Gardens, London Rd.).
- 9 College Green, *c.*1690.
- Wooden water pipes, Folk Museum.
- 17th-century house, St. Mary's Square.

Elegance and Improvement: The Eighteenth Century

In the 1700s, the control of Gloucester was less in the hands of merchants and traders and more under the influence of the local gentry. It was the gentry who usually occupied the two parliamentary seats, and the councillors in the 1700s included gentry and professional men such as lawyers and surgeons. The result was the Gloucester's tiny ruling class was becoming more outward-looking, less parochial. Some took an interest in the current vogue for scientific discovery and ideas of improvement and reform. Gloucester took more interest in national politics; its parliamentary elections were sometimes stormy and bitterly fought. These elections were often rigged by the Mayor and Aldermen. Since only freeholders could vote, it became the practice to create more freeholders at election times in the hope of promoting the Corporation's candidate. This also increased the number of outvoters, freemen who actually lived elsewhere, in towns as remote as Bristol or London. The Corporation's attempts to control elections were by no means always successful. The Tories took both parliamentary seats in 1715 and 1722 and there were riots in 1727 when Whig aldermen attempted to influence the poll by creating even more freemen than usual. After 1734 a civilised agreement was reached by which both parties agreed to share the two seats.

It was good for Gloucester that the gentry took an interest in it, for it helped it to become, in a small way, a social centre. There was a winter 'season' when the rich came to Gloucester: there were assemblies, concerts, and plays (all usually held in the Booth Hall, or in the assembly roms of notable inns like the Bell Hotel). The Three Choirs Festival began in the early years of the eighteenth century. There were houses occupied by the wealthy in the very centre of the town; mansions such as Ladybellgate House, which was built in about 1700 by the Wagstaffe family. It

General view of College Green, 18th century houses. *C. Heighway.*

was occupied in the eighteenth century by the Raikes family, and Robert Raikes, known as a founder of Sunday Schools, was born there. The house has fine plaster-work, some of which displays the swan crest of the Guise family and so was added when the house was tenanted by the Guise family between 1740 and 1743. Rescued from the brink of demolition, Ladybellgate House has been restored by the Gloucester Civic Trust. Bearland House, close by, is of similar date and has also recently been restored. These houses are testimony to the great building boom which hit Gloucester in the early 1700s. Brick came into fashion, and was everywhere used, either to build new houses or to reface old ones: the frontages of St. Nicholas house and 'Winfield's', both in Westgate Street, are excellent examples of the way a new front could be attached to an ancient timber building. Another mark of fashionable Gloucester in the 1700s was the fine gardens which were laid out in the city centre: where the police station now stands there was once an elegant walled garden called Marylebone Park.

Not all the new building was in brick: there was at least one example of a stone building. 'Eagle House', in Westgate Street, built by 1724, and later known as the Duke of Norfolk's house.

Bearland House, early 18th century. The gentry of Gloucester built grand houses in the town centre. *C. Heighway.*

The 11th Duke of Norfolk was a notable character in late-eighteenth-century Gloucester. He was Mayor of Gloucester several times in the last years of the century, and was known for his hospitality. From time to time he would give the Corporation a 'turtle feast', usually at the King's Head, Westgate Street. He was a big, clumsy man, with an aggressive disregard of fashion and indeed of cleanliness. It was said that his servants used to wash him in his drunken stupors, as he would not bear the process when sober. He complained one day to Dudley North that he suffered from rheumatism, and had tried every remedy in vain. 'Pray, my lord,' replied North, 'did you ever try a clean shirt?' The Duke's other claim to fame was that he was responsible for the first Gloucester spa in 1788, when a spring of water, which was said to have medicinal properties, was discovered behind Eagle House. For a while the house attracted fashionable visitors who came to 'take the waters'.

At the other end of the social scale, poverty continued to be a problem which the city leaders had to deal with. There had been bad harvests in the late 1600s and the poor rate had had to be increased and climbed up steadily through the early 1700s. Poor

The Duke of Norfolk's House, or Eagle House, which stood in Westgate Street and was demolished for the building of the 'Dukeries' in 1971. This reconstruction of the house in its heyday is by Phil Moss.

Charles Howard, 11th Duke of Norfolk. The Duke held several Council posts, and was a noted eccentric, being fond of eating and drinking and very averse to washing and to fashionable dress. *Glos. Coll.*

relief was still managed separately for each parish by the parish overseers, supervised by the magistrates, until a committee was inaugurated known as the Guardians of the Poor, which from 1727 received rates and administered relief to the whole city. The Guardians managed the Poor House where the destitute were maintained and set to work, usually on pin-making. The regime in the workhouse was harsh. Even small children had to work long hours; there was supposed to be a school for them but they probably spent little time there. The degrading conditions of the poorhouse were the only recourse for the really poor, but the destitute sons or relatives of freemen did better. There were special charities to pay for apprenticeships for the sons of poor freemen, and the city hospitals took freemen as a priority, then their wives and children; only afterwards were the ordinery poor considered for admission. Even in the hospitals the rules were fairly severe: absence for more than eight days, or misdemeanours such as adultery, could lead to dismissal from the hospital.

The rising poor rate in the early eighteenth century was not accompanied by rising prices, so it looks as if there was a real increase in the amount donated to the poor. Gloucester's poor rate was actually slightly higher than the national average, but it still helped only a minority. Peter Ripley has calculated that between 1710 and 1727 in the parish of St. Nicholas, perhaps 4% of the paupers received allowances from the overseers of the poor, although something like 25% of the population, roughly 1,250 people in the early 1700s, lived near to subsistence level. It was not surprising that people were driven to steal, even though quite minor thefts carried a prison sentence.

The city was obsessed with reducing the numbers of poor by whatever means possible, and it was for this reason that they were so hard on women who gave birth to illegitimate children. These 'lewd women' were sent to detention in the Bridewell for three years and were whipped; in the workhouse the mothers of bastard children were made to eat apart and fed only with leftovers. Women were if possible sent back to their places of legal settlement, leaving the fathers to support the children.

There were plenty of men of means in Gloucester who sympathised with the poor and with those in prison. Robert Raikes ran the local newspaper, the 'Gloucester Journal', begun by his father in 1722. The newspaper was used to promote ideas of reform, especially the improvement of prisons. Robert Raikes, with the Rev. Thomas Stock, were convinced that religious education would steer the poor from a life of crime. Thus the idea of Sunday schools was born. Sunday schools gave not only religious instruction, but also grounding in reading and writing; for many poor children it was the only education they got, for they were often at work the other six days of the week. Sunday schools were meant to be interdenominational, but not surpri-

Rev. Thomas Stock (above) and Robert Raikes, both credited with the founding of Sunday schools. Raikes ran the local paper, the Journal, and used it to further reforming causes. *Glos. Coll.*

singly religious differences arose, and the non-conformists were soon founding their own schools in considerable numbers.

The various non-conformist movements were growing. In the 1600s the Corporation had been orthodox, as a result of Charles II's purges of the Council; in the city as a whole there were only about a hundred non-conformists in 1676 (and one Roman Catholic). Cirencester had a much higher number. One notable non-conformist was James Forbes, who had been a lecturer in the Cathedral in 1654 but was removed at the Restoration. Later he preached in private houses with his American-born assistant, Increase Mather, later a President of Harvard. By the late 1600s some of Forbes' followers had founded the Unitarian church in Barton Street. Another group of Forbes' followers, early in 1730, bought a site opposite the South Gate and built a meeting house there in 1733–4.

The Quakers first made their appearance in the town in 1655 and were constantly persecuted: in 1670 the Mayor and Aldermen closed their meeting house and beat the Quakers with canes. There were not many Quakers: seventeen who were imprisoned in 1682 may have been the total for all Gloucester. By the mid 1700s there were only six Quakers: they belonged to the poorer trades, blacksmiths, gunsmiths. The early history of the Baptists in Gloucester was not dissimilar: there were a handful by 1674, but none by 1735. A Baptist minister died in Gloucester gaol in 1685. The Methodists had far more success: in April 1739, George Whitfield spent a preaching week in the city of his birth: several thousand people attended open-air services, and three or four thousand packed into the Booth Hall to hear him speak. George Whitfield had been born on December 16th, 1714, at the Bell Inn, Southgate Street. At Oxford he met John and Charles Wesley and was profoundly influenced by them. Later he was ordained and preached his first sermon at St. Mary de Crypt. He made seven trips to America, and many American colleges and universities owe their inception to his work.

The non-conformist influence in Gloucester had its part in promoting reform and improvement (there were nine Unitarians on the late eighteenth-century Council). Prison reform was urgently needed. Policing and the administration of justice had become more sophisticated; there were more prisoners than ever before, but prisons were still medieval. The city prisons were the gates, which were insanitary and overcrowded. Prisons were still managed by the gaolers who expected a reasonable return from prisoners to augment their salaries. In 1777 John Howard published his famous report, 'The State of the Prisons'. The North Gate, said Howard, was too small; debtors, felons, and petty offenders were all crowded in together, and there was no courtyard; prisoners had to be exercised on the roof. The East Gate prison, equally unsavory, was demolished in 1780, leaving the North Gate even more overcrowded. In Gloucester was the County Gaol, which was the castle. Here there was only one courtyard and one day-room, into which all prisoners were herded indiscriminately. Howard described the licentiousness of the prisons and reported that several children had been born in gaol. Many prisoners died of infectious diseases like smallpox, or 'gaol-fever' (typhus) which was spread by lice. There was no bath and only one sewer. The prison was so dilapidated that prisoners had to be chained up at night.

The 12th-century castle keep, still standing in the 18th century and used as a prison. It was demolished when the new prison was built in the 1780s. *Glos. Coll.*

The Old City Gaeol, late 18th century, outside the South Gate. Demolished 1862. *Glos. Coll.*

Reform was brought about mainly by the efforts of George Onesipherous Paul, a wealthy aristocrat who had spent much of his enormous fortune on high living and race-horses. In 1780 he underwent a personal change, taking the additional name of George and undertaking good works of every kind. He argued for the proper provision of a prison service as suggested in John Howard's report. He maintained that although prisons should be severe, they should still care for the criminal; most radical, he argued that prison should help bring about the reform of the prisoner. He further argued that a prison sentence should not be equivalent to a death sentence, for at the time there were three deaths from disease in gaol to every execution.

As a result of Paul's efforts, the new county gaol was built at Gloucester on the site of the old one, the medieval castle. It was intended to house 207 men and women, with carefully segregated accommodation. There was more attention to cleanliness, fumigation of clothes, and bedding. Baths were provided for incoming prisoners. The authorities put prisoners to work, in order to 'dispose them to the habits of industry', although productive work was not always easy to find. Convicts would work the treadmill which pumped water into a storeage tank.

Drawing by Captain H.C. Selwyn, dated 1792, showing the approach to Gloucester over Westgate Bridge. *Glos. Coll.*

The prisoners in the gaols and bridewells were there for a variety of causes; the largest number for debt and for theft, often quite minor cases. Gloucester gaol also took political prisoners, such as Kid Wake, from Gosport, who was sentenced to hard labour for five years for shouting revolutionary slogans at George III.

In 1782, a new city gaol was built outside the South Gate, and the old gaol, the North Gate, was knocked down.

Management of the city became more efficient. From 1738 there was a salaried treasurer. Other officers of the city such as bellmen and constables were increased in number. A salaried treasurer had some disadvantages, however, before the city had established machinery to check his activities. An inquiry in the 1780s discovered that the treasurer had considerably mismanaged the city's finances and there were serious arrears: the treasurer was asked to resign. From then on the duties of treasurer were better defined and controlled.

There was reform in the air of politics as well: in the 1780s the Gloucestershire Association was campaigning for an end to the American war and for economical reform. Several prominent members of the Gloucestershire Association represented Gloucester in Parliament.

Other improvements were the new Infirmary, opened in 1761, and the rebuilding of St. Bartholamew's Hospital in the late 1700s. A project for a canal met with enthusiasm, though only the dock was begun: the canal itself had to wait until the next century.

The town environment was also considered. Plans were made to improve the water supply by building reservoirs on Robinswood Hill and conveying piped water to the town. The scheme was however implemented only in the next century, and until then the citizens of Gloucester had to manage with well-water, cisterns, and the old conduits. None of the water was drinkable by today's standards. Street surfaces did rather better: orders for paving became more frequent as the eighteenth century went on. The paving can often be seen today when holes are dug; it consisted of smooth cobbles set in sand; very noisy for carriages, but a great deal cleaner than the former layers of mud. The other disadvantage of the old streets, their size, was also dealt with. Narrow lanes were inconvenient: the fashion was for wide roads through which carriages could easily pass. Many medieval buildings were accordingly demolished as obstructions. The

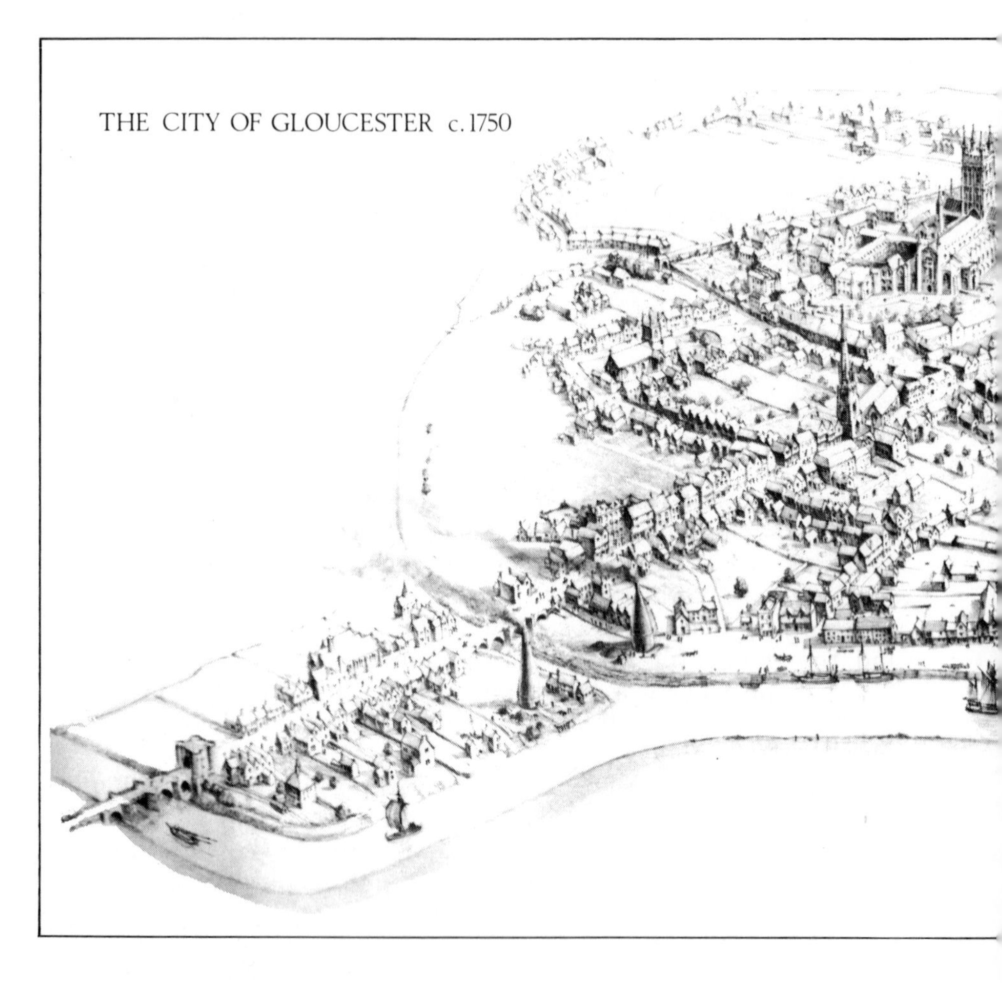

A reconstruction by Phil Moss of Gloucester in about 1750, based on 18th century drawings, old photographs, and a variety of maps including Hall and Pinnell's map of 1789. The conical towers near Foreign Bridge are glass- and

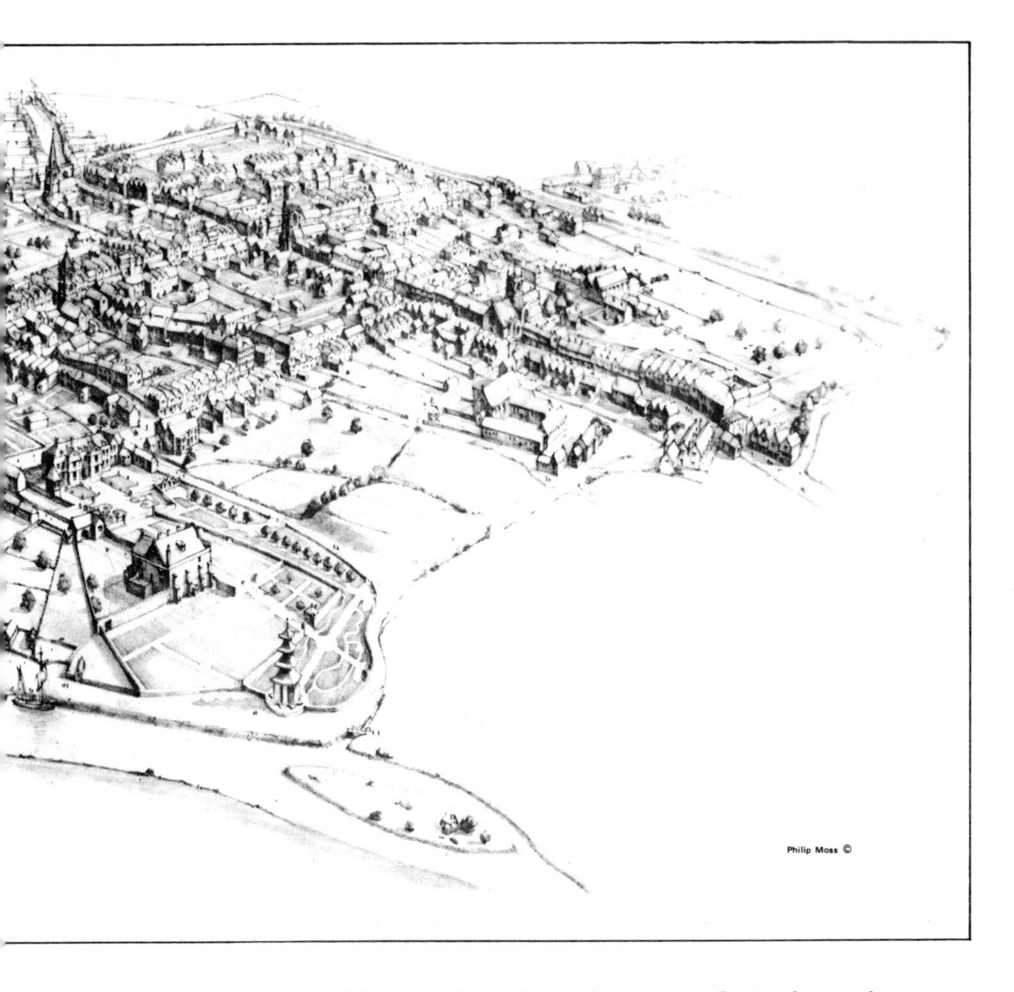

lime-kilns. Note Marylebone Park, with its elegant pagoda, in the castle area. The town is little different in plan and area from what it was in the middle ages.

High Cross, the Kings Board, and the market houses were all demolished, as well as the groups of buildings which since the thirteenth century had occupied the centre of Westgate Street. The East Gate was knocked down in 1780 and the North and South Gates not long afterwards. The West Gate survived longest, being demolished in 1809. In 1824, the historian Counsel remarked, 'Great improvements have already been made . . . in taking down projections and widening avenues in different parts of the city, and many more are in contemplation. We may therefore expect to see Gloucester eventually become one of the handsomest cities in the kingdom.'

Not everyone agreed with this view. There was an antiquarian movement afoot which led Washbourne to publish the original accounts of the Civil War, glorifying Gloucester's past: Fosbrooke produced his 'History of Gloucester', in 1819 and antiquarians such as Lysons made careful records both of discoveries of antiquities, and of old buildings soon to be demolished.

In 1789, a map was made of the city by Messrs Hall and Pinnell (their fee was 10 guineas). By this time, the population of Gloucester was just over 7,000; an increase of about 2,000 over the total a hundred years before. The most remarkable thing about Hall and Pinnell's map is that, in spite of the loss of the gates, it still shows a medieval town, with the ancient boundaries and street lines intact, very small suburbs, and the fields within a few hundred yards of the city centre. It took the canal and the railway, and the energy of the nineteenth century, to expand Gloucester well beyond its medieval boundaries and bring it into the modern age.

EIGHTEENTH CENTURY: WHAT TO SEE

- Many 18th-century houses or frontages particularly in Westgate Street and College Green.

- Ladybellgate House, Bearland Lodge, and Bearland House, Longsmith Street.

- St. John's church, Northgate Street, 1732–3.

- St. Bartholomew's Hospital, late 18th-century: now the 'Westgate Galleria' (next to Sainsbury's Homebase).

- Monument House, St. Mary's Square.

- Gloucester Museum, Brunswick Road: collection of 18th-century furniture.

- Folk Museum, Westgate Street: displays and information on pin manufacture; domestic items; pottery; clay pipes.

- Frontage and pediment of St. Nicholas House, 'The Dick Whittington', Westgate Street.

- Statue of Queen Anne, south side of Gloucester Park (very weathered).

- City arms, carved by Thomas Ricketts, once on old Booth Hall, now on modern wall, west side of Three Cocks Lane.

- Unitarian chapel, Barton Street.

- Parts of Gloucester Prison.

Expansion and Sanitation: The Nineteenth Century

In the nineteenth century Gloucester exploded, both in size and prosperity. In 1800 its boundaries were those of the medieval town; by 1852 Causton's map shows suburbs extending to what is now the inner relief road; by the end of the century it had covered all its fields and overcome its outlying country houses with streets of terraced houses. Its population was 14,000 in 1841, 40,000 in 1871; it had nearly six times more people than 100 years before. This increase had many causes, but one factor was the opportunities presented by new industries, which in turn were promoted by the coming of canal and railway.

The hazards of navigation to Gloucester had been a disadvantage for centuries. Although by the late eighteenth century many canals linked up with the Severn, the stretch below Gloucester could only be navigated for a few days each month on the spring tides. In 1792, a proposal was made to construct a canal. The dock basin was built first and was soon in use for trows bringing coal from the Forest of Dean. After 1809 there was a tram road carrying goods between Cheltenham and Gloucester. The canal, which carried river traffic between Sharpness and Gloucester, was completed in 1827, along with the North Warehouse. The principal imports were timber and corn and the docks were soon flourishing. As the century went on, more warehouses were provided, though in a closely similar style to the earliest ones, and a Mariners Chapel was provided to give the sailors, whose behaviour on shore was often found regrettable, an opportunity to attend church on Sundays. Railway links connected with the docks and enabled incoming goods to be shipped immediately to destinations further inland. A second dock, the Victoria dock, was built by the middle of the century. Although there was a brief fall in trade in the Crimean War, trade was flourishing again in 1860; by then steam tugs, instead of horses, were pulling boats along the canal. Industries connected with the imports were

Gloucester Docks, by Edward Smith, 1878. *Gloucester City Museum.*

attracted to the area: flour mills and oil mills in the dock itself, the Moreland match factory in Bristol road near the dock, and the Gloucester Railway Carriage and Wagon Company, and many more.

In the 1870s the docks at Sharpness were enlarged and improved. This at first created extra trade for Gloucester, but as other docks, at Avonmouth and Portishead, were opened, with better railway links, many cargoes went to the new ports instead. As ships became larger, Sharpness itself became too small for the larger vessels, which could only get into the dock on the higher spring tides each month. Trading conditions for Gloucester then became less favourable. Timber remained a major import, and at the end of the 1800s the timber yards moved further down the canal, where they still are. Most of the buildings round the docks remained in use for the corn trade, and a flour mill is still there today.

The outbreak of the First World War had a disastrous effect on the docks trade and recovery was slow. In the 1960s barge traffic declined still more as a result of the competition from road

Map of Gloucester, 1843, by Causton. The city has spread well beyond its medieval boundaries. *Glos. Coll.*

MAP OF THE
CITY AND BOROUGH
of
GLOUCESTER
FROM AN ACTUAL SURVEY MADE IN 1843

Llanthony Bridge, by Edward Smith 1820–1893. The painting shows the bridge c. 1840, before it was redesigned to swing open. *Gloucester City Museum*, at present in the Guildhall.

transport. Gloucester is still a commercial port, and is also used by pleasure craft. The docks landscape has hardly changed since the nineteenth century, and is a popular location for filming: scenes from the television series 'The Onedin Line' were filmed here.

The railway reached Gloucester in the 1840s, or rather two railways, for there was fierce competition between the different railway companies and the Midland Railway (from Birmingham) and the Great Western Railway (from Swindon) met at Gloucester. Unfortunately the railways were different gauges and passengers always had to change trains at Gloucester. In the end the GWRs broad gauge system was discontinued.

The railway, besides bringing materials and trade to the town and widening its markets, also created new industries. The Gloucester Railway Carriage and Wagon Company became world famous and employed a twentieth of the whole working population of the city in 1871. The firm manufactured railway wagons,

Changing trains at Gloucester, from the *Illustrated London News*, June 6th 1846. The Midland and Great Western Railways, which met at Gloucester, were different guages; and all passengers had to change trains. *Glos. Coll.*

Gloucester Old Bank, Westgate Street, at the beginning of the 19th century. The bank was founded in 1716. The figure in the doorway is the eccentric millionaire banker Jemmy Wood. The site is now occupied by Macdonald's Hamburgers. *Glos. Coll.*

and private carriages for the gentry. Another thousand men were employed in iron foundries and about the same number in the timber trade or manufacture related to it. (Pin making, still strong at the beginning of the century, had almost disappeared by the 1850s.) The enormous increase in building brought employment for many and profits to local builders. The building boom also ensured the prosperity of the timber companies, all situated near the docks. The family with the longest connection with timber were the Prices, later Price and Walker, who were in business in Gloucester from 1736 and were the largest firm in 1900. The firm won a contract to build prefabricated huts for use in the Crimean War, so Florence Nightingale may have visited the sick in a hospital built in Gloucester.

Also flourishing was Gloucester's commercial life, which had its roots in the previous century but with the upsurge in industry had grown still further. The Gloucester Old Bank had been founded in 1716, one of the oldest private banks in England. James Wood, or 'Jemmy' Wood, still ran the bank in Westgate Street in Gloucester in the early nineteenth century. The Gloucester Old Bank survived the difficult time just after the Napoleonic Wars, when many other banks went under: Jemmy himself was a millionaire at his death. Jemmy served on the Corporation of Gloucester, was later Alderman, and twice served as Sheriff. He never became Mayor, perhaps because of the expense – he was notoriously mean. He was also famous for neglecting his appearance. It was said that, one day visiting his property in the country he took a turnip from one of his own fields. He was apprehended by the farmer's bailiff, who whipped him first for stealing and then, when he said he was the landowner, for telling lies. The bailiff was later severely reprimanded.

Another contribution to Gloucester's growth was its Spa. Following the brief success of the Duke of Norfolk's venture, a spring was discovered near the site of the present cricket pitch in 1814, and a Spa Company was formed. Even in the early 1800s the Gloucester spa was hopelessly overshadowed by the far more magnificant Cheltenham, but it still deserves a small corner in its history. A Pump Room was built, and a row of elegant houses which still occupy 'Spa Road'. One of the finest in the row was the Spa Hotel, now part of the Gloucester College of Art and Technology. William Gladstone's parents visited here, as well as many other of the gentry, and for a time the spa was very

Contemporary cartoon showing Jemmy Wood in Hell, preparing to set up partnership with the Devil. The title above reads 'Pandemonium Joint Stock Banking Company'. *Glos. Coll.*

popular, providing public breakfasts and other special events. To provide for the new buildings in the Spa area, a new church, Christ Church, Brunswick Road, was built in 1822 (its brick frontage dates to after 1899).

Gloucester also had other fashionable entertainments, of which the Three Choirs Festival was the most famous. It was claimed in the late 1800s that the visitors in their carriages were seriously inconvenienced by the narrowness of the street leading to the Cathedral porch, so the east side of the street was demolished and a new range of timber-and-brick buildings put in, set back so as to provide a wide avenue to the Cathedral. Some of the large hotels also provided concerts, plays, and balls for fashionable visitors; the Bell Hotel, Southgate Street, saw a concert by Paganini in 1834, although it was very poorly attended. The Kings Head, Westgate Street, was always well-frequented and had been since the early eighteenth-century: Queen Victoria stayed there as Princess.

Gloucester had several theatres at different times: in 1763 there was a new theatre in Barton Street – outside city limits, since the magistrates disapproved of drama. Sarah Siddons played at the Barton Street theatre in 1775, and her daughter was born in Gloucester and christened at St. Michael's church, at the Cross. In 1791 a new theatre was built in Westgate Street, but by 1844 it was let as a warehouse. Behind the Old Booth Hall was the Alhambra Music Hall, but this was burnt down in 1874.

Another source of Gloucester's prosperity were, as in previous centuries, the legal professions which inevitably congregated in the town in attendance on the County Assize Court. In the early nineteenth century a new Shire Hall was built, and new courts added, all by Robert Smirke, designer of the British Museum. A judge is said to have remarked of the new courthouse, 'I can hear everything except the evidence'.

In 1835 the Municipal Corporation Act reformed Gloucester's constitution; the medieval 'burgess' system was abolished and the right to elect councillors given to all ratepayers of three years' standing. The new Corporation had plenty of work in coping with conditions of life in the rapidly-growing city. One of the most pressing problems was the water supply, and by the 1830s the proposals of the late 1700s came to fruition, and there were pipes bringing water from reservoirs on Robinswood Hill. This went to conduits and pumps: the piping of water directly into houses did not start until the late 1800s.

Sanitation also improved beyond recognition in the nineteenth century; in the early 1800s outside closets were still the rule, and even the well-to-do had only chamber pots, often carefully hidden in pieces of furniture or behind screens. Jemmy Wood recorded in his diary the sad day when his favourite cat fell in the closet and suffocated, the lid having been left open. Chamber pots could be very elegantly decorated, but they still had to be emptied into a tub which was collected each night by

Houses in Spa Road: a relic of Gloucester's brief period as a Spa in the first half of the 19th century. *C. Heighway*.

Shire Hall, by Robert Smirke, 1816. *C. Heighway*.

College Street before and after the widening of 1890, which improved access to the Cathedral. *Glos. Coll.*

the night soil men. Water closets did exist but they were rare and special items, and relied on the existence of a nearby stream or drain to take away the contents. In 1848, during a Government inquiry into sanitary conditions, a London official was taken round the town. All the streams were polluted with human, animal, and vegetable waste; privies often drained into cesspools which seeped into the streams. In Northgate Street there was a tub left for privy waste which was regularly emptied into the open gutter, and a slaughter house in Southgate Street also emptied its waste into the gutter.

By now it was well-known that such conditions caused disease. In 1848 a new public health act was passed making it obligatory for each house to have a fixed sanitary arrangement of some kind; either an ash-pit, or privy, or water closet. The Board of Health map of Gloucester, drawn in 1852, plots all the privies in Gloucester. Some of these are occasionally dug up by archaeologists, who may then enthuse over the collection of broken chamber pots, 'willow pattern' pottery, discarded shoes, and lost hairpins. In the late 1800s a system of brick sewers was beginning to be built, and only then was it possible for water-closets to be introduced in greater numbers, and for public conveniences to be opened.

Another important requirement for public health was public baths, and these were opened in Gloucester in 1886.

Epidemics of infectious disease were by no means a thing of the past in nineteenth-century Gloucester. In 1832 there were 123 deaths from cholera (which results from infected drinking water): an isolation hospital was converted out of a house in the city fields along Barton Street. Scarlet fever was another killer; there were 178 deaths in 1882. An isolation hospital in the Stroud Road area had been set up, but it was not very effective; more people died in it than out of it. By now vaccination against smallpox was possible, but the vaccination programme lapsed in the 1880s and in 1895–6 there was a severe smallpox epidemic. Schools were closed, and social events cancelled. A re-vaccination programme was introduced.

The Gloucester Infirmary had existed since the mid 1700s. At first it occupied the Crown and Sceptre Inn in Westgate Street. A new Infirmary was opened in 1761 outside the Southgate; it was intended for 'the care of the sick or lame of any County or Nation who are destitute of the means of support'. Not surprisingly, the hospital was often over-crowded, necessitating patients sharing beds.

Horton Road Hospital; the County Insane Asylum, completed in 1828. The provision of an asylum was part of a much more humane attitude towards the insane, who had in the past often been chained up in prisons. *Bill Meadows.*

It had been intended to add to the hospital a wing for the insane. The condition of these unfortunate people, who were often confined in workhouses in terrible conditions, had long concerned reformers. In 1823 an asylum in Horton Road was opened and supplies were ordered of equipment such as strait-jackets and hand-cuffs. Gradually the harsher treatment which these items imply was done away with. Dr. John Baron, one of the physicians, a friend and biographer of Jenner, had a practice in Gloucester and was one of those who saw that reasonable comfort and good diet were more important than restraint and punishment.

Sickness was a double disaster for ordinary working people; though they might be cared for the hospital, neverthless there was no insurance for loss of earnings; there was no sickness benefit and anyone taken ill or injured would simply lose their

Terraced Houses in the Lower Barton Street area. These were the better housing for workers in the late 19th century. They were all built on the same plan, with slight variations: two rooms downstairs and two up, with a washhouse and outside privy at the back. Modernized, these are comfortable homes. *C. Heighway*

The new cemetery created in the 19th century when the increase of populaltion meant that burial in city churches had to cease. The cemetery chapels are by Medland, 1857. *C. Heighway*.

Southgate Independent Chapel, built 1851, demolished 1983. *Glos. Coll.*

Baptist chapel and school, Brunswick Road, built in 1821. It was rebuilt in 1872–3, and demolished in 1974. Its site is now the Co-operative Store. *Glos. Coll.*

Bluecoat Hospital, Eastgate Street, 1886, by R. Curzon. The Bluecoat School was originally founded in 1666 by Sir Thomas Rich and was rebuilt in 1807. It was demolished in 1878 to make way for the Guildhall. *Gloucester Museum.*

job. The result might be the workhouse for the whole family. Working hours were long and hard; in the wagon works there was a week of 54 hours, reduced to 53 in 1895. Many people were crowded into the old slums of St. Mary de Lode and St. Aldate parishes, where living conditions were particularly poor and the mortality rate high. The average life span in the 1840s was about 30, the same as in medieval times, and the infant mortality rate was still very high; about half all the burials in St. Mary de Lode parish in the 1840s were of children. With the improved conditions of the late nineteenth century, the mortality rates improved, and the population consequently increased still more. The terraces of brick houses to the east and north of the city represent improved living conditions for workers, as well as indicating the enormous area the city covered by 1900.

Another consequence of the high population was the lack of

A horse tram at the top of London Road. Horse trams were introduced in 1878. *Glos. Coll.*

space to bury people in. The city churchyards had long since reached capacity, and a government ordinance of 1855 forbade further burial in crowded city graveyards. Land was accordingly purchased in the fields outside the city to the east, and a municipal cemetery was started with chapels designed by the well-known local architect, Medland. It was consecrated in 1857.

Non-conformists had become a substantial element in Gloucester: the Methodists were especially numerous. The non-conformists were particularly active in the various reforming movements, being strong supporters of Sunday schools and the temperence movements. Within the established church life still continued on its old pattern, maintaining comfort for a few, often based on pluralism, and over-small stipends for many curates. The 'reforming' wing of the church, the Evangelicals, had found a supporter in Gloucester when the evangeligal Henry Ryder was appointed as Bishop. Ryder turned his attention to many committees which were trying to reform the church system and improve the stipends of the poorer clergy.

Southgate Street in the late 19th century. *Glos. Coll.*

The town's expansion meant that the city churches and parishes, dating in both cases from the twelfth century or before, were unsuitable; the parishes were re-organised to adapt to the new population areas. Many churches were built in the new suburbs, both Anglican and non-conformist. There were more schools too; a National School opened in 1815 and a Poor School opened in 1813 for 200 boys. The Blue Coat Hospital (Sir Thomas Rich's School) was rebuilt in the early 1800s. Primary Schools were built after the Act of 1870 empowering local authorities to set up primary schools for all children. In 1897 the City Library was opened. After 1835 the first professional city police force for the city was begun. Gas lighting first appeared in 1819, although it was very inefficient at first and in 1823 the 'extensive and commodious works for the making of gas', near the Quay, had to be rebuilt. The lighting functioned better thereafter. By 1864 there were horse-drawn buses; horse-drawn trams appeared in 1878. Electric trams were to be introduced in 1904. By that time, if by some twist of time a medieval Gloucesterian could have paid his town a visit, he would find it hard to recognise. The Cathedral, a few buildings, the outline of the streets, would be the only familiar features of the townscape.

Barton Fair, 1882; the fair was held in Eastgate Street. *Glos. Coll.*

NINETEENTH CENTURY: WHAT TO SEE

- Docks (guided tours available – see Information Centre).

- Custom House, Commercial Road 1845.

- Folk Museum, Westgate Street: domestic equipment and everyday life; also agricultural material.

- Transport Museum, Barbican Road, Longsmith Street.

- Churches: St. Mary de Lode, nave; rebuilt 1823. All Saints, Barton Street 1875 (by Gilbert Scott); Christ Church, Brunswick

Road 1822; Mariners Church, Docks 1849; St. Mark, Kingsholm Road 1847; St. Paul, Stroud Road 1882–3; St. Peter, London Road 1860–8 (Roman Catholic); St. Stephen, Linden Road 1895; Cemetery chapels (by Medland) 1857.

- Chapels: Congregational Church, Lower Barton Street 1874–5; Friends Meeting House *c.*1840; Whitefield Presbyterian Church, Park Road 1871.

- Public Buildings: Shire Hall, Westgate Street 1816; Guildhall 1890–2; Eastgate Street Market (portico only) 1856; Museum 1897–1900.

- Over Bridge, by Telford (visible from western approach to Gloucester).

- Almshouses, Wotton Pitch, London Road.

- College Street, east side (by Waller) 1890.

- Hooper Monument, St. Mary's Square 1862.

- Worcester Street, early 19th-century.

- Lloyds Bank Eastgate Street 1898.

- National Provincial Bank *c.*1889.

- Clarence Street, early 19th-century.

- Spa Road, early 19th-century.

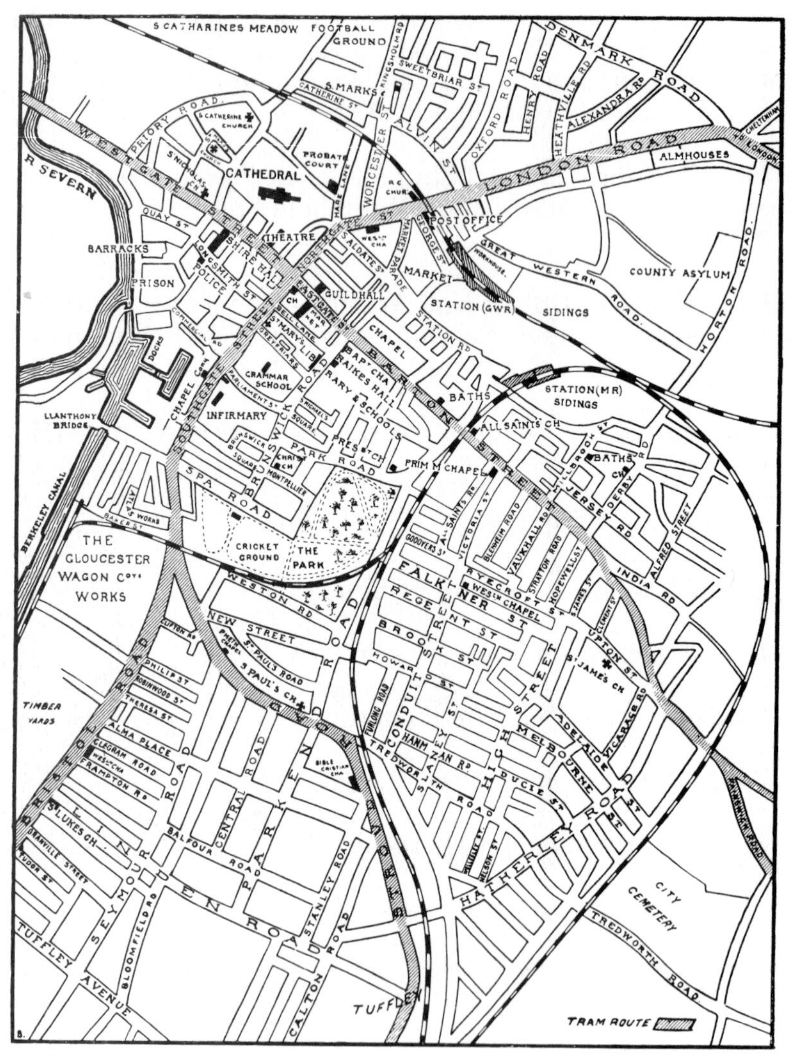

Map of Gloucester, from 'The Borough Pocket Guide to Gloucester' 1904. The expansion of the suburbs is well under way. *Glos. Coll.*

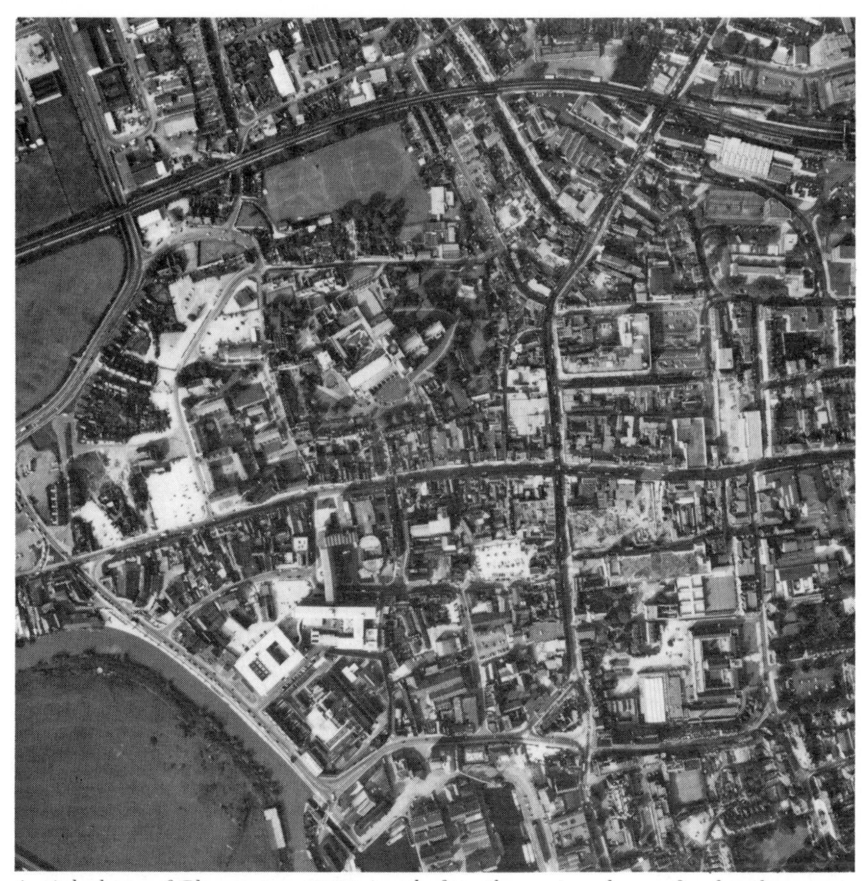

Aerial photo of Gloucester, 1968, just before the major phase of redevelopment. The medieval street pattern can clearly be seen, and is not much changed today. The outline of the castle can be seen in the bottom left corner of the town, and the curve of the Roman fort ditch to bottom right. *Air Photograph Division, Cambridge: crown copyright reserved.*

Epilogue: Modern Gloucester

Gloucester's industries continued to grow and diversify in the twentieth-century. For many years and especially during the Second World War, Gloucester was famous for its aircraft, which today are commemorated in sculpture in a garden behind the Museum. As the amount of motor traffic grew, the streets became inadequate, and a Ring Road was created and some streets widened in the 1930s. Otherwise Gloucester still had a medieval scale even until the 1950s. This impression was enhanced by the presence in the town of the livestock market, once in King's Square and later on the site of today's bus station: plenty of Gloucestrians today can remember cattle being driven through the streets. The redevelopment of Gloucester in the late 1960s and 1970s has re-shaped nearly a quarter of the town centre, and banished the cattle market to St. Oswald's Road, west of the city. Many industries and commercial firms have moved to Gloucester and it has grown to a population of 90,000, overwhelming its neighbouring villages. Its population includes immigrants who have added their own individuality to Gloucester's streetscape: the domes of two mosques now rise above Lower Barton Street.

The loss during the re-development of many old buildings prompted much public protest, and ironically created more awareness of the town's past. Today Gloucester is a thriving shopping centre, and is more conscious of its heritage than it has ever been. There is an exciting scheme afoot for the revival of Gloucester Docks, the City Council even moving its own offices there. The town has come in for much criticism for destroying its past, but time does not stand still. What is more, that past can still be seen, both in the pattern of the streets and in buildings, which survive from Roman, Saxon, medieval, and later times. Gloucester's 2000 years of history have left their mark on the town of 1985.

Northgate Street, c. 1970. A good example of a misleading streetscape. The black-and-white house was built c. 1936. The small shop to the left was Southern's stores, 3 Northgate Street. Behind its uninspiring brick front was a late 15th-century town house, discovered too late to avoid demolition in 1972. The destruction of 'Southern's' became something of a rallying cry for many citizens unhappy about the destruction of old buildings. Gloucester Civic Trust was formed not long afterwards.

A drawing by Phil Moss showing 3 Northgate Street as it would have looked in the 15th century.

Oxbody Lane ('The Oxbode') before its redevelopment in the 1930's: a reminder that not all radical change is a product of recent decades. The demolished street includes several medieval buildings. In medieval times this was one of Gloucester's poorest areas. The black-and-white building glimpsed in the distance is 20th century. The adjacent photograph shows the same view today. *Glos. Coll. and C. Heighway.*

ost
fice
Gas

Gloucester today: a view from Eastgate Street towards the west. The Guildhall is on the extreme right. The street curves where it was diverted from its Roman line to pass through a ruined Roman building. On the left is the 14th-century tower of St Michael's church. *Bill Meadows.*

Principal Sources

Abbreviations: GRO Gloucester Record Office
GBR Gloucester Borough Records (GRO)
TBGAS Transactions of the Bristol and Gloucestershire Archaeological Society.

Articles and books mentioned more than once are listed at the end of this summary.

ROMAN, pp. 1–17

The Iron Age background is dealt with in A. McWhirr, *Roman Gloucestershire* (1981), and Salway 1984, p. 83. * The fort at Kingsholm is fully published in Hurst 1985. * For the fortress at Gloucester see Hassal and Rhodes 1974, Hurst 1972, Hurst 1974, Hurst 1976, and for the East Gate, Heighway 1983a. * Roman cemeteries: C. Heighway, 'The cemeteries of Roman Gloucester', *TBGAS* 98, 1980, pp. 57–72, and Hurst 1985. * Roman tilery: C. Heighway and A. Parker, 'The Roman Tilery at St. Oswald's, Gloucester', *Britannia* 13, 1982, pp. 97–149. * Roman house under Telephone Exchange, Berkeley Street: Hurst 1972 and 1974. * Mosaics: D. Neal, *Roman Mosaics in Britain*, 1981, pp. 82–86. * Mosaic under St. Mary de Lode Church: Bryant 1980. * Roman public baths: Hurst 1972, 1974; Heighway and Garrod 1980. * Roman gates and defences: Hurst 1972, 1974; Heighway 1983a. * Roman riverside wall: Garrod and Heighway 1984, p. 3. * Recruitment of soldiers in Salway 1984. Name of Gloucester: M. Gelling, *Signposts to the Past*, 1978; English Place Name Society, vol. xxxix, Part II, p. 124. * Town area as defined by cemeteries: Hurst 1985, pp. 131–3. * Pottery: Ireland et al. in Heighway 1983a. * 2nd-century bank at Gloucester: Hurst 1973, p. 29. * Account of end of Roman Britain: Salway 1984. * Subdivision of baths in Gloucester: Heighway and Garrod 1980. * Early 4th-century defences: Hurst 1972, 1974; dated in Heighway 1983a. * For worsening climate see D. Hill, *Atlas of Anglo-Saxon England*. 1981, p. 9. * Gloucester house surviving to early 5th century: Hassal and Rhodes 1974. * End of Roman Gloucester in Hurst 1976 and Heighway 1984a, 1984b. * Replanning of city centre, early 5th-century: Heighway and Garrod 1980. * Kingsholm warrior burial: Hurst 1985. * Manuring of urban land: Heighway 1983b. * 5th and 6th-century pottery and smiths' tools: T. Darvill, 'Excavations on the early Norman castle at Gloucester', *Medieval Archaeology*, forthcoming.

BRITISH TO SAXON, pp. 18–28

* Background referenced in Heighway 1984a, 1984b, 1984c. * 'Conan' mentioned in Gildas: *The Ruin of Britain*, ed. and trans. M. Winterbottom 1978, p. 30, and note, and 'Conmail' in Whitelock 1961, year 577. * St. Mary de Lode church, sub-Roman: Bryant 1980. * The annal for the year 577: Whitelock 1961. * Founding of Gloucester Abbey: H.P.R. Finberg, *Gloucestershire Studies*, 1957, pp. 12–61; *Early Charters of the West Midlands*, 1972, pp. 153–66. * New line of Westgate Street: Heighway and Garrod 1980. * Wooden objects: Heighway, Garrod and Vince 1979. * 9th-century cross-shaft from St. Oswald's Priory: Heighway 1980.

TENTH-CENTURY NEW TOWN, pp. 29–38

* Annal for the year 914: Whitelock 1961. * Date of Gloucester streets: Hurst 1972, p. 67; Heighway 1984a and b. * Berkeley Street: Garrod and Heighway 1984, p. 48. * St. Oswald's Minster: Heighway 1978 and 1980a. * Kingsholm Palace: Hurst 1985. * All this chapter appears in more detail in Heighway 1984a and b.

CASTLE AND ABBEY, 1066–1200, pp. 39–61.

* Castle: Hurst 1984. * 'Tables' set: I. Stewart and M.J. Watkins, 'An 11th-century bone tabula set from Gloucester', *Medieval*

Archaeology 28, 1984, pp. 185–9. * Norman East Gate: Heighway 1983a. * St. Peter's Abbey: Verey and Welander 1979. * Land taken from St. Oswald's Priory: Heighway 1984a. * Royal Palace at Kingsholm: Hurst 1985. * Endowments to Abbey in late 11th-century: C. Brooke, 'St. Peter of Gloucester and St. Cadoc of Llancarfan', in *Celt and Saxon: Studies in the early British Border* 1964; D. Bates, 'The Abbey of St. Peter's Gloucester and its early Norman benefactors', *TBGAS* 102, 1984, pp. 129–32. * Gloucester Candlestick: *English Romanesque Art, Exhibition Catalogue, 1984, p. 249* (the candlestick is actually copper alloy with a very high silver content). * The 'Gloucester family': D. Walker, 'Miles of Gloucester, Earl of Hereford, *TBGAS* 77, 1958; 'Charters of the Earldom of Hereford', *Campden Miscellany* xxii (4th S. vol 1), 1964. * Stone castle: Hurst 1984. * Roman quayside wall and Lower Quay Street: Garrod and Heighway 1984. * Llanthony Priory: Page 1907. * Llanthony records: I. Jack, 'An Archival Case History: the Cartularies and Registers of Llanthony in Gloucester', *Journal of the Society of Archivists* 4.5, 1972, pp. 370ff. * 12th-century St. Oswald's Priory: Heighway 1978. * State of streets deduced from archaeological evidence: see Garrod and Heighway 1984. * Charters and town management: Reynolds 1983. * 11th-century economy: Heighway 1984a, 1984b and forthcoming.

THIRTEENTH CENTURY, pp. 62–78

* Mureage account of 1298: Gloucester Record Office, GBR 1307/1361. * Mureage in general: H. Turner, *Town Defences in England and Wales*, 1971. * Eastern defences of Gloucester: Hurst 1972, Heighway 1983a. * Gates, especially west gates: Hurst 1974, M.H. Ellis, 'The Bridges of Gloucester', *TBGAS* 51, 1929, pp. 169–210. * For the Fulbrook stream see L.E.W.O. Fullbrook-Leggatt, 'The River Twyver and the Fullbrook', *TBGAS* 83, 1964, pp. 78–84. * For a full description of medieval streets see Fullbrook-Leggatt 1952. Identifying medieval side-streets is not easy, and interpretations differ. Compare, for instance, Lobel 1969, Langton 1977, and Fullbrook-Leggatt 1952. Most interpretations are based on the 1455 Rental, for which see Stevenson 1890. * Castle: Hurst 1984. * Troubles of 1263–5: W.A. Wright, *The Chronicle of Robert of Gloucester*, 1887. * Religious orders of Friars: Page 1907. Blackfriars: Page 1907, W.H. Knowles, 'Black Friars at Gloucester', *TBGAS* 54, 1932, pp.

167–201. * Roof of Blackfriars: O. Rackham, W.J. Blair and J.T. Munby, 'The 13th-century roofs and floor of the Blackfriars Priory at Gloucester'. *Medieval Archaeology* 22, 1978, pp. 105–22. * St. Peter's Abbey building history: Verey and Welander 1979. * St. Oswald's rebuildings: Heighway 1978. * Fires recorded in Abbey chronicles: W.H. Hart, *Historium et Cartularium Monasterii Sancti Petri Gloucestriae*, vol. i, 1863. * Quote about fire of 1300 in Hart, p. 35. * Banning of thatch: Lobel 1969. * Tanners Hall: Heighway 1983b. * Ceramic tiles: Vince in Heighway 1983a, p. 214. * Life and trades in 13th-century Gloucester: Lobel 1969. * Eyre of 1221: F.W. Maitland, *Pleas of the Crown for the County of Gloucester*, 1884.

FOURTEENTH TO FIFTEENTH CENTURY, pp. 79–97

* Trade and economy, 14th and 15th centuries: N. Herbert, '1483: Gloucester's Livelihood in the Middle Ages' in *The 1483 Charter in History*, 1983; N. Herbert (ed.), *History of the City of Gloucester, Victoria County History of Gloucestershire*, vol. iv, forthcoming; Lobel 1969; Waters 1983. * Rental of 1455: Stevenson 1890. * Abbey buildings and history: Verey and Welander 1979. * Other buildings: Verey 1970. * Monastic Life: Verey and Welander 1979 and Waters 1983. * Chantries: N. Saul, 'The religious sympathies of the gentry in Gloucestershire 1200–1500', *TBGAS* 98, 1980, pp. 99–112. * Town life: Waters 1983. * State of defences in 1487: HMC, pp. 406–7. * 1483 charter: Reynolds 1983.

SIXTEENTH CENTURY, pp. 98–118

* Account of visit of Henry VIII: HMC, pp. 443–4. * General background, G. Baskerville, *English Monks and the Suppression of the Monasteries*. * Dispossessed monks: G. Baskerville, 'The Dispossessed Religious of Gloucestershire', *TBGAS* 49, 1927, pp. 63–122. * Fate of monastic buildings: Lobel 1969, Heighway 1978. * Gloucester benefactors: B. Frith, *Twelve portraits of Gloucester benefactors*, 1972. * Education: N. Orme, *Education in the West of England 1066–1548*, 1976. * Protestants in 16th century: K.G. Powell, 'The Beginning of Protestantism in

Gloucestershire', *TBGAS* 90, 1971, pp. 141–57. * Bishop Hooper: F. D. Price, 'Gloucester Diocese under Bishop Hooper', *TBGAS* 60, 1938, pp. 51–151. * Death of Hooper: G. Townsend, ed, *The Acts and Monuments of John Foxe*, VI, 1946, pp. 636–62. * Ecclesiastical Commission of 1574: F.D. Price, 'The Commission for Ecclesiastical Causes for the Dioceses of Bristol and Gloucester, 1574. *TBGAS* 59, 1937, pp. 61–184. F.D. Price (ed.), 'The Commission for Ecclesiastical Causes in the Dioceses of Bristol and Gloucester 1574', *Bristol and Gloucestershire Records Section* vol. X, 1972. * Thomas Powell, Chancellor of Gloucester: F.D. Price, 'An Elizabethan church official: Thomas Powell, Chancellor of Gloucester Diocese', *Church Quarterly*, April–June 1939. * Counter-reformation and Thomas Alfield: P. McGrath, 'Gloucestershire and the Counter-Reformation in the reign of Elizabeth I', *TBGAS* 88, 1969, pp. 141–63. * Literacy: trade and economy: Clarke 1979. * Family size: Laslett 1984. * Horse Pool: Heighway 1983a. * Streets, cleaning and other council orders; references in Council Books: see subject index to GBR in GRO. * Pound for pigs: HMC, p.470. * Bridewells described in J. Whiting, *A House of Correction*, 1979. * Other details of social life in Clarke 1979. * Deaths from plague: Ripley 1972. * Government of Gloucester: Clarke 1979.

SEVENTEENTH CENTURY, pp. 119–133

* Causes of Civil War: Laslett 1984. * Puritanism among Gloucester rulers: Clarke 1974. * Siege of Gloucester: Washbourne 1825; J.R.S. Whiting, *Gloucester Besieged*, 1975. * Flooding of meadows: Washbourne 1825, p. 387. * Refusal of City to surrender: Washbourne, 1825, p. 44. * Quote about 'granadoes' from Dorney's account of the siege, in Fosbrooke 1819, p. 36. * State of Westgate drawbridge and defences: HMC, p. 505. * Quotes about labour of garrison, repair of fortifications: Washbourne 1825, p. cxxi. * Gloucester accounts of provisions sent to Cromwell: Washbourne 1825, p. 425. * Cathedral under the Commonwealth: S. Eward, *No Fine But a Glass of Wine*, 1985. * Celebrations of 1660: Fosbrooke 1819, p. 61. * Purge of Councillors after Restoration: Ripley 1977. * Work and economy in 17th-century: Ripley 1976, Ripley 1977 and Clarke 1979. * Streets: entries in GBR (Council Books and Account Books).

EIGHTEENTH CENTURY, pp. 134–149

* Elections: Clarke 1979, Clarke 1984. * Ladybellgate House: M. Rogers, *Ladybellgate House, Gloucester, and Robert Raikes*, 1975. * Duke of Norfolk: information from M/S by Brian Frith, 'Duke of Norfolk and Gloucester City', in GRO. The anecdote about the shirt, pointed out to me by Mr. Frith, is in the *Dictionary of National Biography*. * Streets: entries in Council Books, GBR. * Religious movements from Ripley 1977. * Prison Reform and George Onesipherous Paul: Whiting 1975. * Demolition of gates in Council Books, GBR, and in Heighway 1983a. * Poor rates, state of poor: Ripley 1977 and 1980. * Raikes, Stock, and Sunday schools: Laqueur 1976. * Northgate gaol described in Howard, *State of the Prisons*, 1790, p. 328. * Demolitions in city recorded in Council Books, GBR. * Officials, and city government: Clarke 1984. * Late 18th-century politics: J. Cannon, 'The Parliamentary Representation of the City of Gloucester 1727–1790', *TBGAS* 78, 1959; J. Cannon, 'Gloucestershire Politics 1750–1800', *TBGAS* 79, 1960, pp. 293–97. * For inns and aleshouses: A. Dodd and P. Moss, *Gloucester Alehouses*. 1985.

NINETEENTH CENTURY, pp. 150–171

* H. Conway-Jones, *Gloucester Docks*, 1984. * The rest of the chapter is based mainly on a series of supplements published with the Citizen in 1983. Part IV (April); Theatre, by Brian Frith; Part V (May); The Spa and other entertainments, by Brian Frith; Part VI (June); plagues and epidemics, by Bryan Jerrard; Part VII (July); Health and Hospitals, by Brian Frith; Part IX (September); Transport, by Roger Whiting. Part XI (November); Commerce, by Bryan Jerrard. * Other sources: Horton Rd. Hospital: A. Bailey, 'An account of the founding of the First Gloucestershire County Asylum', *TBGAS* 90, 1971, pp. 178–91. * Early 19th-century improvements: G.S. Blakeway, *The City of Gloucester: its Royal Charters of Liberties and varying fortunes*, 1824 and G.W. Counsel, *History of Gloucester*, 1829. * Jemmy Wood's diary: I. Gray, 'Jemmy Wood's Journal', *TBGAS* 90, 1971, pp. 158–77. * Jemmy Wood anecdotes: C.H. Savory, *Life and Anecdotes of Jemmy Wood*, 1882. * Sunday Schools: Laqueur 1976. * Police:

B. Jerrard, 'Early policing methods in Gloucestershire', *TBGAS* 100, 1982, pp. 221–40. * Ryder, Bishop of Gloucester: W.J. Baker, 'Henry Ryder of Gloucester 1815–24', *TBGAS* 89, 1970, pp. 130–44.

ARTICLES AND BOOKS MENTIONED MORE THAN ONCE

Bryant, R, 1980. 'The church of St. Mary de Lode, Gloucester, *Glevensis* 14, pp. 4–12.

Clark, p. 1979. 'The Ramoth-Gilead of the Good: Urban Change and Political Radicalism at Gloucester 1540–1640', in P. Clark, A.G.T. Smith, and N. Tyacke (eds), *The English Commonwealth 1547–1640.*

Clark, P. 1984. 'The Civic Leaders of Gloucester 1580–1800' in P. Clark (ed), *The Transformation of English Provincial Towns.*

Fosbrooke, T.D. 1819. *An Original History of the City of Gloucester* (reprinted 1976)

Fullbrook-Leggatt, L.E.W.O., 1952. *Anglo-Saxon and Medieval Gloucester.*

Garrod, A.P. and Heighway C.M. 1984. *Garrod's Gloucester.*

Hassal, M. and Rhodes, J. 1974. 'Excavation at the New Market Hall, Gloucester, 1966–7', *TBGAS* 93, pp. 15–100.

Heighway, C.M. 1978. 'Excavations at Gloucester: fourth interim report; St. Oswald's Priory', *Antiquaries Journal* 58, pp. 103–32.

Heighway, C.M. 1980a. 'Excavations at Gloucester: 5th Interim Report: St. Oswald's Priory', *Antiquaries Journal* 60, pp. 207–26.

Heighway C.M. 1983a. *The East and North Gates of Gloucester.*

Heighway, C.M. 1983b. 'Tanners Hall, Gloucester', *TBGAS* 101, pp. 83–110.

Heighway, C.M. 1984a. 'Anglo-Saxon Gloucester' in J. Haslem (ed), *Anglo-Saxon Towns in Southern England,* pp. 359–83.

Heighway, C.M. 1984b. 'Anglo-Saxon Gloucester to AD 1000', in M. Faull (ed), *Studies in Late Anglo-Saxon Settlement,* pp. 35–53.

Heighway, C.M. 1984c. 'Anglo-Saxon Gloucestershire' in A. Saville (ed), *Archaeology in Gloucestershire.*

Heighway, C.M., Garrod, A.P., and Vince, A.G., 1979. 'Excavations at 1 Westgate Street, Gloucester 1975', *Medieval Archaeology* 23, pp. 159–213.

Heighway, C.M. and Garrod, A.P. 1980. 'Excavations at nos. 1 and 30 Westgate Street, Gloucester', *Britannia* 11, pp. 73–114.
HMC. Historical Manuscripts Commission, *12th Report, Appendix ix,* p. 419ff.
Hurst, H. 1972. 'Excavations at Gloucester, First Interim Report', *Antiquaries Journal* 52, pp. 24–69.
Hurst, H. 1974. 'Excavations at Gloucester: Second Interim Report', *Antiquaries Journal* 54, pp. 8–52.
Hurst, H. 1976. 'Gloucester: Glevum: a Colonia in the West Country' in Branigan K. and Fowler, P.J., *The Roman West Country*, pp. 63–80.
Hurst, H. 1984. 'Gloucester Castle', *TBGAS* 102, pp. 73–128.
Hurst, H, 1985. *Kingsholm.*
Langton, J. 1977. 'Late medieval Gloucester: some data from a rental of 1455', *Institute of British Geographers Transactions* N.S. 2.3, pp. 159–77
Laqueur, T.W. 1976. *Religion and Respectability.*
Laslett, P. 1984. *The World We Have Lost: Further Explored.*
Lobel, M. 1969. 'Gloucester' in *Historic Towns Atlas,* vol. i.
Page, W. (ed). 1907. *A History of the County of Gloucester,* vol. ii (Victoria History of the Counties of England).
Reynolds, S. 1983. 'Gloucester and Town Government in the Middle Ages' in *The 1483 Charter in History.*
Ripley, P. 1972. 'The Parish Register Evidence for the population of Gloucester', *TBGAS* 91, pp. 199–206.
Ripley, P. 1976. 'Trade and Social Structure of Gloucester, 1600–1640', *TBGAS* 94, pp. 117–23.
Ripley, P. 'The Economy of the City of Gloucester, 1660–1740', *TBGAS* 98, pp. 135–54.
Ripley, P. 1977. *The City of Gloucester 1660–1740,* University of Bristol thesis.
Salway, P. 1984. *Roman Britain.*
Stevenson, W.H., (ed.) *Rental of all the houses of Gloucester, by Robert Cole,* 1890.
Verey D. and Welander, D. 1979. *Gloucester Cathedral.*
Washbourne, J. 1825. *Bibliotheca Gloucestrensis.*
Waters, G. 1983. *King Richard's Gloucester.*
Whiting, J.R.S. 1975. *Prison Reform in Gloucestershire 1776–1820*
Whitelock, D. (ed.) *Anglo-Saxon Chronicle.*